PTSD
WORKBOOK

Self-Help Techniques for Overcoming Traumatic Stress Symptoms.

ANTHONY RUSSELL

Table of Contents

Introduction

This book will shed light on the topic trauma. Trauma is a disorder, which makes a person depressed and agitated about certain events. Trauma can be of many types. It can be psychological trauma, physical trauma and physiological trauma. Trauma has symptoms as well and it can be cured through proper medication and a flexible routine of exercises. The longer we live, the more unavoidable it is that we will encounter injury. Injury is the reaction to a profoundly upsetting or upsetting occasion that overpowers a person's capacity to adapt causes sentiments of defenselessness, reduces their feeling of self and their capacity to feel the full scope of feelings and encounters.

It does not segregate and it is unavoidable all through the world. A World Mental Health overview led by the World Health

Organization found that in any event 33% of the in excess of 125,000 individuals studied in 26 unique nations had encountered injury. That number rose to 70% when the gathering was restricted to individuals encountering center issue as characterized by the DSM-IV (the arrangement found in the Diagnostic and Statistical Manual of Mental Disorders, fourth Edition). Yet, those numbers are only for occasions that have been accounted for; the genuine number is most likely a whole lot higher.

While there are no target criteria to assess which occasions will cause post-injury side effects, conditions normally include the loss of control, selling out, maltreatment of intensity, defenselessness, agony, disarray as well as misfortune. The occasion need not ascend to the degree of war, cataclysmic event, nor individual attack to influence an individual significantly and adjust their encounters. Awful circumstances that reason post-injury side effects differ significantly from individual to individual. Surely, it is exceptionally abstract and it is imperative to manage at the top of the priority list that it is characterized more by its reaction than its trigger.

Regular Responses and Symptoms of Trauma

Reaction to a horrible accident changes fundamentally among individuals, yet there are some essential, basic indications.

Enthusiastic signs include:

- bitterness
- outrage
- forswearing
- dread
- disgrace

These may prompt:

- bad dreams
- a sleeping disorder
- trouble with connections
- passionate upheavals

Normal physical side effects:

- sickness
- discombobulation
- changed rest designs
- changes in hunger
- migraines
- gastrointestinal issues

Mental issue may include:

- PTSD
- sorrow

- uneasiness
- dissociative issue
- substance misuse issues

Intense Stress Disorder versus Post-Traumatic Stress Disorder

Few out of every odd damaged individual creates post-awful pressure issue (PTSD). A few people build up certain side effects like those recorded above, however they leave following half a month. This is called intense pressure issue (ASD).

Sorts of TraumaWhen the side effects last over a month and truly influence the individual's capacity to work, the individual might be experiencing PTSD. A few people with PTSD don't show indications for quite a long time after the occasion itself. What's more, a few people manage PTSD side effects of an awful encounter for an amazing remainder. Indications of PTSD can heighten to fits of anxiety, sadness, self-destructive considerations and emotions, medicate misuse, sentiments of being detached and not having the option to finish every day assignments.

Sorts of Trauma

As referenced above, injury is characterized by the experience of the survivor. Be that as it may, there is an outline of injury levels. Extensively depicted, they can be delegated huge 'T' injuries and little 't' injuries.

Little t TraumasSmall 't' injuries are conditions where one's real wellbeing or life isn't undermined, however purpose side effects of injury in any case. These occasions set coincidental kilter and upset typical working on the planet. They unquestionably do not appear to be little at all when they happen, yet most will have a simpler time recouping from them than an enormous 'T' injury. Then again, little 't' injuries are once in a while ignored since they appear to be surmountable. This can be risky as the combined impact of a natural injury or injuries may trail an individual persistently. Models are: life changes like a new position or moving; relationship occasions like separation, treachery, or an upsetting individual clash; life stressors like money related issues, work pressure or struggle, or fights in court.

Huge T TraumasLarge 'T' injuries are unprecedented encounters that achieve extreme pain and weakness. They might be one-time occasions like demonstrations of psychological oppression, regular calamities, and rape. Or on the other hand, they might be drawn out stressors like war, youngster misuse, disregard or brutality. They are considerably more troublesome or even difficult to ignore, yet they are frequently effectively maintained a strategic distance from. For example, individuals may avoid triggers like individual updates, certain areas, or circumstances like swarmed or even abandoned spots. What's more, they may oppose standing up to the memory of the occasion. As a method for dealing with stress, this works for such a long time. Drawing out access to help and treatment drags out mending.

Chapter 1 – Know trauma

This chapter will talk about trauma in detail that what it is about and what are the related concepts of it

Stories of trauma

Shan's Story

On 28th January 2015 at roughly 6.30pm I was associated with a mishap, which was to change my life until the end of time. Propelled by others that have shared their accounts before me on the AfterTrauma site, I am composing this article with the expectation that my story can likewise give you the mental fortitude and self conviction through the beginning times of recovery.

All that I recall is leaving work to go to a delight treatment arrangement at 6pm. I called my significant other from the vehicle as I generally do, and review taking a gander at the check in the vehicle and recall that I was running 10 minutes ahead of schedule for my arrangement. I don't have any memory of occasions after that until I woke up 8 days after the fact in Southampton Intensive Care Unit, startled and mistook for my family close by. The occasions paving the way to this have been filled in by my family, companions, specialists at the shop where I was before the mishap and the nursing staff at Southampton Hospital.

Obviously, it was a virus however dry night, the sky lit by the moon. I was passerby, going across a little town street to my vehicle, which was left in a little lay-by, arranged on a street that associates two towns. I was sporting dark, accepted to be by the side of my vehicle yet the driver didn't see me. He didn't stop straight away however fortunately turned around as he suspected he had hit something.

My advisor, Kayleigh, heard a blast similarly as I had left the shop and watched out towards her vehicle that was left in a similar lay-by. She saw that her windscreen had been crushed. Going to the call the police, Kayleigh and her partner headed outside and met with the driver who said he thought he had hit a person or thing. My advisor saw that my vehicle was still there and my tote was in the street. They discovered me on the opposite side of her vehicle in the forest. I had been hit by the voyaging vehicle and had arrived on her vehicle, before arriving in the lush clearing.

I had endured numerous and complex wounds with damage seriousness score of 64 out of a potential 75 and given a 6.1% possibility of endurance. My wounds included breaks to my neck (C2), back (L1 and L5), broken shoulder, shoulder bone, elbow, each rib, some with numerous cracks, broken pelvis and 2 broken legs. (The break in my left leg had been missed and not recognized until 5 months after the fact). I likewise had inward wounds to my lungs and a pancreatic drain. The specialist treating me for my lungs and said that in his 30 years of training, he had just observed comparable rib harm in Afghanistan, treating officers harmed in bomb impacts. My wounds were broad and my forecast at first poor, yet the medicinal group set up me together adequately to start the voyage which I currently can tell.

My significant other was called to the scene and was with me preceding the crisis administrations showing up. Having been treated at the scene by a paramedic, while trusting that the specialist and emergency vehicle will show up, I was then taken to Southampton General A&E - the Major Trauma Center for our district. Obviously, I was cognizant – talking and attempting to get up off the floor. On requiring the crisis benefits the workers at the shop had addressed the inquiries used to survey my condition – this we accept may have influenced the prioritization of the rescue vehicle and the police-it was additionally 'change after some time.

The A&E group at Southampton were prepared for my appearance and worked quickly on me. My family depict the circumstance at the time as mistaking for little data from the get-go. My wounds were with the end goal that my family were advised to expect the most noticeably terrible during the initial 48 hours however I dismantled through to be all around ok to have the 7 hour activity on the Friday 30th January. The family were informed that my circumstance was possibly life finishing and on the off chance that I survived I would have a long recuperation.

Roughly 8 days after the fact I woke up in Southampton ICU amazingly mistook for a pipe stuck down my throat, with my family who had not walked out on me. I review the most distinctive dream. I thought I was in a rich lodging gathering and hearing voices I thought were the receptionists and visitors. The fantasy hosted included a supper get-together at our home with companions, trailed by my better half endeavoring to 'cut the house down' encompassed by US troopers who had lost arms and legs. There were 2 Indian looking women present – one of which had dark and gold spotted face who was calling me to security. I know now that to be my little girl Stephanie who never walked out on me. Stephanie has spots on her temple - these were the gold and dark dabs that I saw on one of the Indian women.

The photo underneath was a 'glad' day - the fourth February 2015 - the day I woke up and had the breathing cylinder extricated. My better half imparted this to me the prior night I left emergency clinic 3 months after the fact as I was feeling discouraged - I utilize this photo presently to glance back at how far I have come.

I was exceptionally startled just as confounded and urgent to recognize what was happening and where I was. I couldn't convey because of the pipe and was offered a pen and cushion to record my inquiries, which were obscured clearly. I heard a ton of voices, discussion and individuals crying. I thought at one point I had been determined to have terminal malignancy and recall requesting that my better half be straightforward with me. I currently realize this crying to be guests of one of the patients in the narrows by me who had kicked the bucket subsequent to ending his own life. It appeared to require some investment before I could get any understanding of what had occurred, why I had something stuck down my throat. I nearly felt that individuals were not being straightforward with me – either that or I simply didn't understand and was befuddled.

In the 10 days I spent in Southampton General I got the most brilliant expert consideration from the specialists who worked on me and spared my life, the great attendants and my family and dear companions, some of whom remained at the medical clinic and took it in goes to sit close by. My little girl seems to have directed a great part of the action and facilitated loved ones visits and guaranteed that the medical caretakers were 'on it'! She and the attendants grew a solid bond. Regardless I feel the blame of putting my family through such stress and upset.

The prescription pulled some shocking pranks on me and I review the torment, particularly when I was moved in my bed. In any case, I recollect affectionately the hair washes, interminable creaming and the adoration and care given by the attendants - I particularly recall my medical caretaker Sally who had a 'pack of cream' that she had purchased with her own cash to use on patients. I recall ambiguously being sat up without precedent for the 'Barton' seat and having a hair wash. I thought I was moved to a zone with no dividers, which neglected the ocean - obviously I had not left Bay 2! I love hearing the commotion of the ocean. The physio began very quickly – OMG the agony the first occasion when I sat on the edge of the bed … however to Fiona (physio) I will consistently be thankful. Physio turned into my closest companion and still is.

Correspondence has assumed a significant job in my recovery - both great, awful and aloof. Its absence and regularly the manner by which it was conveyed has caused numerous issues. In spite of being told by the clinical experts that my stay in Southampton was at least 3 weeks because of the intricacy of my wounds, and guaranteed it was the 'best spot' for me, at roughly 7.45pm on the Friday sixth February we were educated I was being released and moved to Basingstoke Hospital. This was a troublesome and mistaking time for myself and the family. In the long run, at about 11pm that night we were informed that the move was not occurring as it was excessively cold and late to move me until the next week.

The following day, Saturday seventh February, I was moved to Basingstoke HDU by rescue vehicle, alongside my medical caretaker Sally and girl Stephanie. Befuddled and concerned, I was welcomed anyway by a well disposed group and invited into what was to be my new home. The memories of HDU were inadequate experience of staff in moving me and disarray as to my relief from discomfort when conceded. My contextual investigation was utilized in the as of late distributed NICE rules on Trauma - I am satisfied to state that Communication was distinguished as one of the 5 key components affecting the treatment of significant injury.

While there were some correspondence issues, there were likewise a few regions that functioned admirably for me during my recovery. These included having the help of a Trauma Coordinator Nurse who composed issues and came to refresh me every day with respect to what was happening. This key job was acquainted as of late with help upgrades in the help of Trauma treatment in the UK.

Something I expected to do was to 'plan'. I need to design - that is the manner by which I tick. I can review meeting my first specialist in Basingstoke and approaching him for an arrangement and he advised me that I was a called a 'tolerant' and that was for motivation.... 'to show restraint'. Nobody could give me that arrangement that I longed for to continue accepting that I could vanquish this unpleasant thing that had transpired. I had to know when I could walk, when I could next move, jump on a plane to the sun, return to work. a month and a half in nonetheless, I was fortunate enough to have the most superb advisor in Nigel Rossiter who facilitated my consideration and treatment. Not just has he given me master treatment and care, he has given me the chance of being somewhat of a national hero for injury and I have exhibited my story inside the NHS, both broadly and locally with the expectation that I can carry a distinction to other injury patients - my method for returning something.

I was fortunate enough to have private medical coverage as one of my work benefits and was moved into the private wing of the emergency clinic late February 2015 and made it my home until my release the 30th March 2015. I was not able weight bear and dependent on care every minute of every day. Be that as it may, my significant other made me a room down the stairs alongside the essential hardware provided by the OT office. We were truly individually! We attempted the consideration framework however this was not prepared for somebody who required every minute of every day care. For the initial 7 months of me coming all the way back my significant other didn't come back to work and remained at home to think about me. I don't have a clue what I would have done if this had not been conceivable.

A significant achievement for me was the thirteenth April when I was given the green light to weight hold up under and from that point forward I have been figuring out how to walk and building my stamina and wellness with hydrotherapy, physiotherapy and visits to the rec center. Everybody supporting me has given me the most astounding consolation and commendation with respect to my advancement - this has given me considerably more assurance. Truth be told, I have define an objective to be fitter than previously - however haven't set a timescale!

I have discovered that the mental recuperation of injury, positively for my situation, ought to be handled before during the recovery. Family ought to likewise have support. I endured glimmer backs, loss of rest and extremely low minutes - despite everything I do so now. I presently have a dread of exceptionally boisterous motor clamors and always stressed over recollecting being hit. I likewise had the extra challenge of not coming back to my job as HR Director. This was a hard for me however I have utilized it as a chance to accomplish something that my family advised me, that I had needed to do even before the mishap and set up my own HR consultancy business, called Liverty HR. I named the organization after a little vessel I found in Barbados on the commemoration of my mishap. It signifies 'vitality of life'.

Be that as it may, the help from my clinician when I got it has been amazingly useful. I have returned to the area of the mishap, Southampton ITU and Basingstoke HDU as a major aspect of my mental recovery. The other thing that helped me was the huge help I had from family, companions, work associates and even individuals that I didn't have the foggiest idea - the quantity of cards, messages and guests were amazing. This truly gave me the quality that I expected to traverse the beginning periods of my recovery.

As a component of my 'arranging' and to anticipate an energizing future, during my time in medical clinic, with my little girl, who was continually close by, we set up together a container list. The highest priority on the rundown was an occasion to our preferred spot, Barbados - we have recently returned - every one of the 10 of us! Additionally one of different occasions on my basin rundown was a 'Remaining Alive Party' which was hung on the fifteenth August. Held in our nursery, loved ones from work, companions from our nearby town just as a portion of the therapeutic experts helped me to celebrate remaining alive. It was my method for saying thank you for the kinship and bolster they had given to me and my brilliant family. What a night we had!

Having an organized recovery plan and thinking about a portion of the help accessible to me prior in my recovery it would have had an enormous effect. Perusing other individuals' accounts has given me the motivation to continue onward and see the promising end to present circumstances.

I remain everlastingly obliged to the magnificent NHS, the experts, specialists, medical caretakers, physios and my loved ones for giving me the help and support to get to where I am today. On account of crafted by the medicinal experts and philanthropies out there, significant advancement has been made in the treatment of injury patients in the UK. A portion of those upgrades presented for example blood given at scene, I know spared my life and have made my recovery much simpler. Be that as it may, we have to continue making contrasts by sharing our encounters. For data, these are the territories that I talk about in my introduction:

- Present the mental help and remember the family
- Expel administration inside the framework and arrange assets
- Recovery plan post release and set up national injury focuses
- Teach managers

I am told I have an additional a year of recovery before I am 'fixed'. I may never appear to be identical, or be as versatile, however with the help of my family and that exceedingly significant self assurance and conviction, I am accomplishing things since I could never had envisioned and opposing all the chances. 2016 will be an incredible year, celebrated with our little girl's wedding in July and setting up my own business.

Evi's Story

Howdy. My name is Evi and I'm 36 years of age. Just about two years prior, on the 13 August 2015, I was engaged with a genuine street auto collision.

I don't recollect how it occurred and I am thankful for that. The police revealed to me that there was a pot opening out and about which got my front side wheel of my vehicle and range me into inverse heading, where my vehicle unfortunately hit another vehicle at a joined speed of 100 mph.

All I recall was awakening in the vehicle and everything was in a very moderate movement, in outright tranquil. No feeling of smell or contact, just nothingness. At that point the adrenaline kicked in and I needed to drag myself out of the vehicle since I could smell smoke. Still not realizing what had occurred and where I was. The main thing I knew was that my legs weren't working and that I would not like to consume.

I was taken to St George's Hospital, Major Trauma Center. I was terrified as I was in so much agony and stupified from all the painkiller drugs. There were bunches of specialists, medical caretakers, signaling clamors, tubes, numerous inquiries tossed all toward me, a large number of voices that didn't sound good to me. I had no clue why I couldn't feel my legs and what wasn't right with me.

I went through two months in St George's. Consistently was a fight for me, particularly as

I don't originate from this nation, I am from the Czech Republic, so I didn't have my family around.

It was a hard two months. All my poise was no more. I turned out to be absolutely subject to everybody around me. I needed to figure out how to confide in outsiders rapidly. Their decisions, proclamations, counsel and trust me it wasn't in every case simple.

Be that as it may, then again, I additionally had a stunning help from the awesome treatment group, who assisted with my recovery. The clinical attendant pro, who was the correct hand of my specialist, consistently put a grin all over. There was likewise the doorman, the supper woman and housekeeper with her tremendous eagerness forever. Meeting different patients and hearing their accounts additionally helped and caused me to acknowledge how fortunate I was and that it could be more terrible, which turned into my day by day mantra. Every one of these individuals and their joined exertion made me work twice as hard so their diligent work wouldn't be squandered.

Having the option to be in contact with my family by means of web was pivotal, and my astonishing companions that came to see me and help got me through my emergency clinic remain.

Two months down the line I returned home. To be straightforward I was petrified to go. For me it implied leaving my "wellbeing net", my "new home" and the new companions I had made. I was leaving to return home, which was around then in the center of no place, and where I lived with my ex-accomplice, so not the friendliest encompassing. I was not permitted to weight uncovered for a half year and all I truly needed was to fly back home to my family yet proved unable.

I didn't tell anybody how startling the idea of leaving medical clinic was for me, as everybody around was so bright and glad for me to arrive at that objective of leaving, so for what reason to be terrified, right?!! I was readied. We had drilled. So I went, said my farewells and gigantic expressions of gratitude.

One month subsequent to being at home I arrived in a desperate predicament. The scariest thing is I didn't see it coming, since that was not me. I am ordinarily a constructive individual, the glass is full. The littlest undertakings like getting to a restroom in a wheelchair, or putting my washing on.

Not in any case that, just to accumulate the garments for washing was a tremendous undertaking. The agony and steady weariness all of abrupt turned into my constant friend.

Likewise my area wasn't perfect, and companions having their own families and occupations to do couldn't visit as regularly as they trusted. I turned out to be desolate and secluded. I turned out to be sincerely and physically depleted. To the point that I could see no chance to get out and just idea it may be better for everybody around if there was no me. At that point, exactly right then and there I got a green light for flying and could fly back home. Where I permitted myself rest and wasn't the only one any longer.

From that point on, I felt careful about any awful emotions. I was later determined to have a PTSD. I likewise needed to have an activity on my arm for the nerve damage harm and experience another activity on my pelvis as the screws had begun to give me issues. Practically following a year from the mishap I could scarcely sit or stand up without torment. Yet, my last activity was last November and from that point forward I've been feeling good.

I engaged in a few patient commitment ventures, planning to help other people with my experience and story. There is in no way like gathering, finding out about somebody who experienced a comparative thing and gaining from them that indeed, there will be good and bad times, mishaps, yet it truly improves.

I am still in recuperation, basically due to my arm and nerve wounds now, yet in May I did a cyclethon ride for Barts Charity to fundraise for injury look into and to bring issues to light. It was energizing for me to have the option to bicycle once more. I swim again and have begun to work three half days seven days. Regardless I get depleted rapidly am as yet getting neuropathic torment yet, I am figuring out how to deal with that through a wide range of treatments, reflection, breathing systems. I found another man in my life, who is amazingly understanding and strong and who doesn't see my scars. I have extraordinary loved ones who helped me when I required it most

I am alive gratitude to stunning group of specialists, attendants, advisors, loved ones. I can never express gratitude toward them enough. I will always remember the sentiment of having a shower just because, heading off to the loo myself, my initial step (which I cried and giggled about simultaneously with bliss) the first occasion when I could brush my hair with my correct hand. I have figured out how to esteem my scars as they recount to my story, I acknowledge the amount I've found out about myself and my very own quality. Also, I trust the peruser will realize that it truly improves, persistence, fearlessness, diligent work and time.

David's Story

I am a multi year elderly person (in 2019) who had a Traumatic Brain Injury (TBI) matured 45 in July 2015 because of an impact between a vehicle and my bike.

The mishap was in Nantwich, Cheshire - I was taken by Midlands air rescue vehicle to be treated at the North Staffordshire emergency clinic. Upon affirmation, my mind was worked on and I was more than once surveyed as having a Glasgow Coma Scale (GCS) of 3 (serious) during the accompanying two weeks, where I was in a 'characteristic' at that point instigated extreme lethargies. At the point when I left the lethargic state, I had 'Secured Syndrome' for seven days.

I was released from medical clinic following a further couple of months, and afterward acknowledged I was setting out on the 'genuine adventure' of recuperation. In June 2016, I began to do deliberate jobs, at that point in July 2017 I had the option to come back to paid work in my previous job with the Metropolitan Police administration as an IT security advisor. I have my expert site where you can see a greater amount of my experience and even a video of me displaying at a gathering.

These days I am chipping away at low maintenance independent premise, however am progressively associated with deliberate business related to mind injury recuperation with the NHS and restorative colleges in the UK.

I've expounded much on my TBI experience on a site I set up together. I've seen that accidental perusers locate the landing page depiction of my damage and beginning of hospitalization of generally intrigue. In any case, as a TBI survivor I discover the recuperation areas additionally intriguing and envision most TBI survivors would do in like manner. My recuperation has been named 'professional recovery', as I discovered genuine reason and fulfillment in my child ventures towards typicality by doing different volunteering jobs. This methodology wasn't arranged - it simply occurred, and worked truly well for me. I'd prescribe it to any individual who needed to increase a sentiment of direction in life subsequent to enduring injury.

Cissy's Story

Scores of recollections, not stirred to, yet set up by onlookers resuscitating their own recollections.

The day started with my typical movement in New Orleans. Visit common court first, at that point come back to the 51st floor law office. I would return with the company's lawyer who held up two roads over in his SUV to help bring document stepped shows, shading pictures and pages of contention reworking the case's ceaseless story. These pleadings I put into conveying request, behind me in a truck, too rich to even consider being basically held and strolled.

On the morning of that date, October 23, 2014, a huge white truck slammed from behind, sending me out of sight. After I fell, in one road circumscribing the town hall, a nearby group assembled, outside witnesses, and furthermore including those from court having seen this through the windows. Two police officers drew nearer from where they worked downtown on steeds, at that point both a fire engine and emergency vehicle showed up, having been called by the police. One police officer got off to compose a ticket, yet couldn't totally depict the circumstance since it became important to expel me, the oblivious lady, by rescue vehicle to University Hospital Emergency, found downtown near to us. The truck driver drove himself into tears. He had admitted to the police that he came up short on any protection. This need did not concern me, since I was grinding away when the mishap happened, and specialist's pay protection concerned me. The association's protection paid for me altogether, from in-patient to out-quiet status. The law office was not able endeavor recuperation of any assets from the man's non-existent protection.

My better half landed at University Hospital from his government court hearing, subsequent to being told of the mishap. The government hearing was proceeded for a considerable length of time. My significant other was not permitted to see me, until emergency clinic workers could clean their new patient. In any case, he said he mystically watched his better half before the tidy up was really wrapped up. I wore emergency clinic garments, not wicked and remaining before him showing with hands and outward appearances not to stress. He didn't in certainty go into my space for 60 minutes, after he encountered this vision-like appearance, and I was not cognizant when he did at last observe me. The entirety of my suit garments, watch and rings had been expelled to the clinic's protected. The staff experienced life-sparing methods, keeping me taking in a head-spread with oxygen going through my nose and throat. This turned into a difficult night, at that point a few evenings, during the greater part of which he in the end returned home. Our child joined day by day subsequent to being rejected from work.

The principal night, my better half mentioned his significant other's gems, and was told she ought to request that herself when capable. Knowing this official exhortation to be doubly unlikely - who thought about her endurance or her physical and mental capacities following that. He requested a medical clinic worker and a gatekeeper on obligation to accompany him to help recognize, and sort out his better half's close to home things, so he could guarantee and expel them. He took his child that night for the first of their numerous café meals. Expression of these troublesome occasions spread through Dallas, New Orleans and somewhere else, to family, work-places, companions from chapel and synagogue, all offering their passionate solace, petitions, visits.

[In my own awareness, I had a dubious capacity to watch some of what befell me. My separation was outrageous, and appeared to me inhabited by my perished mother. I detected her solid support for me to remain alive.]

My two weeks at University Hospital spared my life however not my reasonableness. My better half needed to search for another recuperating medical clinic and restoration offices since University offered no such administrations. Life became for that office breathing and the capacity to swallow, yet those beds and staff constantly anticipated the following dangerous crisis. After a transition to a nearby uptown medical clinic, during recuperation for me as in-persistent, a recovery search was made by my better half all through Louisiana and Texas. What appeared to be a wonder to him in his enthusiastic frenzy, and was a positive astonishment to other relatives, the uptown office interceded to offer me their own out-understanding recovery offices. Near my home neighborhood, they had demonstrated to be my mending medical clinic, and afterward they offered ensuing recovery specialists, attendants and advisors.

I gradually stirred, irregularly, in the emergency clinic during in-persistent recuperation, in November and December of 2014. I previously perceived guests other than my better half and child. They originated from my work-place, individuals from the sea legitimate office. Just a single lawyer, my mishap day partner, did I totally review, while for other people, I required names, depictions. In any case, my recognition of this lawyer is that we had a long discussion, until it turned out to be obvious to him that I talked drivel. I thought we were having an entertaining trade, snickering, however he left saying "great night, until some other time." At least he would return.

I realized that recovery would concentrate on out-quiet capacities I may accomplish following close lethal physical hits to my head and to one side of my body. Treatment would address cerebrum damage coming about because of my skull crack. My psychological aptitudes would be tried by discourse and neuropsychological masters. My physical developments should improve through exercise and rec center machine treatment.

As an in-quiet remaining medium-term in my room at the medical clinic, I gulped thick fluid with complete uneasiness, however it was given to me for wellbeing. I was told I would stifle on slight fluids, however I felt oppositely, that thick ones tasted severe and hindered my throat. I sneaked tap when I utilized my room's latrine, and had guests walk me by foyer drinking fountains. My bathroom entryway was before long bolted except if I expected to utilize it, generally with assistance. Wellsprings stayed accessible for me, with guests.

I understood I was gradually preparing for an arrival to customary life. Two language teachers worked with me to express my considerations, to accomplish for myself a comprehension of such musings. I working on going all over stairways with nurture staff, frequently with my significant other and child who likewise tossed balls to me over the rooftop's volleyball-type net. In any case, I additionally rested a decent arrangement, as per companions' reports. "Each opportunity I come you are sleeping!" kept in touch with one. Strolls close by to nibble on hamburgers and French fries with guests were upbeat trips for me, yet objected by the medical clinic. With dinners in the clinic or anyplace, I looked physically just as I never ate. Medicinal staff needed to tube-feed me. My significant other demanded that I "please eat," under such conditions, and I pursued his requests. Some weight returned.

My Dallas family, not routinely observing me, didn't know the amount I had recouped nor how much assist I with stilling required. They concocted plans for me to pursue other than recovery, either remaining with them or in a living-helped home, since they trusted me to be harmed hopeless. Just in December when I sat rapidly up in bed, talking boisterously and ordinarily to my meeting sibling, did he perceive my"self." "There she is," he said to a medical attendant. This was the point at which he understood that my in-persistent hospitalization was about finished. The following stage would start for me, when I landed at restoration from my home. My discussions with restoration staff started just before Christmas, the week family anticipated me, my child and spouse to make occasion travel to Texas. I had consented to a

"Recovery Attendance Contract" and I began that program December 22.Meeting with me, the dim haired neuropsychologist looked just as he suspected me brimming with rubbish. I portrayed encounters, for example, nation visits 90 miles east of Dallas, and excursions by private plane to Cancun with school companions. By our next session, he appeared to trust I had spoken "truly"of these occasions.

I met every day after Christmas, from 9 am until 3 pm, with the neuropsychologist in his office overseeing and observing mental testing and our dialogs, with a language instructor for oral and perusing practices in her office, and with numerous athletic physical mentors and their gear in the rec center. I invested a lot of energy in the kitchen and the close by found patient parlor with a restorative recreational person. She discussed her work in numerous different zones of the emergency clinic. Her timetable with me concentrated on working me once more into the city network, by presenting an assortment of exercises, in the kitchen cooking with different patients, out together at lunch, shopping together for kitchen supplies, playing games. I didn't completely comprehend her social objectives. I felt an individual objective: get back midtown to work. As recovery time passed, just the language instructor appeared to remember my own objective. Numerous different patients had been in this recovery program for a considerable length of time, potentially being relied upon to remain for a few more.

My language teacher trained me word-discovering techniques, for utilizing when I couldn't state the correct word at the correct minute. It helped me to remember school, substituting equivalent words with comparable implications for words, regardless I utilize this strategy when I become disappointed imparting and attempting to state or portray something. "Vehicle" for trip, "type" for letter, "grin" for joke, not constantly suitable, yet needed rapidly. This specialist had me perused portions of papers and portray or expound on their implications, yet in the end we were examining paper articles about city occasions, neighborhood races. She left to take a new position, and revealed to me that it may be the ideal opportunity for me to complete recovery also.

Rec center specialists empowered riding stationary bicycles, voyaging stairs and strolling passages, lifting loads, resting in positions for extending. I brought home an attracted exercise program to proceed, knee to chest, stomach propping, lumbar preparing, developments natural to me. After restoration, I utilized the program at home, and regularly at my exercise center.

Grace's Story

On second April 2014, my entire world was flipped around, never to be the equivalent again. I was associated with a RTA which has transformed myself from numerous points of view, for eternity. I pledged 2 years back that on the off chance that I at any point discovered life after injury, I would do all in my capacity to pass that expectation on to other injury survivors... so here I am.

I don't recollect the day of my accident. I don't recall a great part of the month a short time later either truth be told. Obviously, I was driving home alone from my accomplice's home, while in transit to purchase my dad a birthday present – a typical day right? For an obscure explanation on that adventure, down a street I went on every day, once in a while two times every day, my traveler wheel crashed into the nearside control, sending me onto the contrary side of the street and into the way of an approaching vehicle. Obviously, my vehicle moved onto its rooftop, I was halfway launched out and caught by my safety belt as the vehicle slipped over my lower body. Fortunately no different gatherings supported any physical wounds.

I had a RSI at the scene (Rapid Sequence Intubation), which is the place they put you off to rest and place a breathing cylinder in to ensure I could inhale alright before going on the ventilator. I was acquired by means of HEMS I + V with pelvic cover and spinally immobilized. I was a 'Code Red Trauma Call' at St George's Hospital in Tooting, which implied I was taken to CT examine then directly to theater for crisis medical procedure. It was since the degrees of my wounds were affirmed. I had broken a sum of 28 bones in my body, incorporating into my neck, skull, spine, arm, pelvis, ribs and hip. I had 'de-gloved' my correct lower arm and thigh which implies that each layer of skin had been detached. My spleen was dying, my kidneys were coming up short, my lungs had been punctured and I had broken my liver. It was additionally discovered the following day that piece of my entrail had gotten ischemic and subsequently some portion of it was expelled and I was fitted with an ileostomy pack for 5 months. I was additionally shrouded in consumes from the petroleum in the vehicle.

(On the image above, I should include that I additionally had a "diffuse axonal head damage" my physio who made the skeleton just disclosed to me he neglected to include it!)

I at that point went through 22 days in GICU in an incited trance like state, before venturing down to HDU and afterward the injury orthopedic ward for a further 62 days. I had a metal 'in-fix' around my pelvis, which implied that I wasn't permitted to weight uncovered for 12 weeks, and lost a great deal of bone and muscle quality in that time. I dropped two stones in weight in 3 weeks, and I wasn't permitted to weight uncovered through my correct arm for half a month in the wake of awakening either. That was a very testing 3 months, yet what I didn't know was that it would get a mess more terrible before it improved.

I don't recollect any of my time on GICU, and my first recollections post-mishap were up on the ward. The last I recollected was the 31st March, at this point it was around the tenth May... I will always be unable to portray that it is so difficult to grapple with not recalling an entire month of your life, particularly when you give day in day a shot to recollect what occurred. I had been in a virtual world for a month, imagining the strangest, wackiest dreams, which I was resolute were reality.

In the long run with the help of family, companions and the stunning staff at St George's Hospital, I began to comprehend that none of these things were genuine, and that I had been in an instigated unconsciousness which implied I had some solid medications in my framework. Step by step I started to acknowledge what had occurred, and things became more clear, including the degree of my wounds and scars – I still right up 'til today don't recollect the mishap.

Consistently was a battle. I'd gone from complete freedom to having a catheter, a stoma, a sustaining tube, a trickle and a murmur for a voice. I couldn't go to the latrine, feed or wash myself. It was in any event 2 months before I even had a shower and I understood the amount we underestimate the 'seemingly insignificant details'. I was so reliant on everyone around me and that was amazingly troublesome. I was encompassed by stunning help as medical attendants, human services aides, word related advisors, physiotherapists, drs, specialists, dieticians, physcologists, language instructors, loved ones. They all pushed me every day and kept my spirits high in the most troublesome a great time, and for that I will always remember every single individual.

I was released home on 26/06/2014 however went through the following two months all through my neighborhood clinic and St George's before I had my ileostomy switched in September 2014, when I at that point got a frightful episode of pneumonia. 'When is this going to end' I pondered internally. I directed such an extensive amount my idea and emotions into my wounds, especially my ileostomy sack, that I truly thought I was Ok rationally. It was in September 2014, when I was released home, that reality hit and I was a long way from OK. I couldn't eat. I couldn't rest. I couldn't grin. I couldn't talk. I couldn't sit in front of the TV. I couldn't chuckle. Everything I could do was cry. I went 72 hours without resting at one phase. Indeed, even now, when I recall how I felt then around then, I get mournful... It's an inclination that you can't depict except if another person has felt it. I tumbled to my mom's feet in the lobby one morning, not long after I'd been released and beseeching her to reveal to me I would have been OK, that I would recover a real existence and crying that in the event that this is the manner by which I was going to feel always, at that point I would not like to live. I truly could see no chance to get out. Not long after I was determined to have melancholy and summed up uneasiness issue.

At this stage I began taking an energizer, which empowered me to recover a type of schedule, in that I could shower or eat without crying and I could rest for in any event a few hours. As I began to feel better inwardly, I began to show signs of improvement physically too on the grounds that I had the drive and inspiration to do as such. I set myself another objective consistently, from the outset it would be to 'stroll to the restroom' at that point 'stroll to the washroom and back' and these advanced to 'strolling as far as possible of my street with only a mobile stick' or 'doing my make up with my left hand' in light of the fact that my correct hand had serious outspread nerve harm and I couldn't utilize it. These objectives kept my going every day, except there is consistently that vulnerability. I expected to see someone who had experienced the equivalent physical injury and was OK now.

Regardless of what number of individuals let me know 'you'll be fit again in a matter of moments', I expected to see that it had been done to realize that it was conceivable, on the grounds that I had no trust in my capacity at all.

Toward the finish of November 2014 I was confessed to Queen Mary's Hospital for about fourteen days of extraordinary physiotherapy. I went into the medical clinic as a wheelchair client, strolling close to 200metres with a mobile stick and a limp. Inside 10 days of recovery, I ran my first 5KM on the medical clinic treadmill in quite a while. I needed to get this under 40 minutes thus the day I was released I ran another 5KM in a short time. It was the first run through in quite a while that I saw I could recover my life. It totally changed my life everlastingly and I will always remember that minute. It hurt, it was extreme and I was in misery a short time later… yet I did it and that sentiment of elation a short time later exceeded any agony. It was here that I set my present moment and long haul objectives to keep me advancing through my recovery. My definitive objective was to run the London Marathon by 2019. Following quite a while of not having the option to utilize my legs appropriately, I just envisioned that one day they would bear me 26.2 miles London.

I continued advancing with my running, while gradually recovering my life on track — coming back to uni, going on vacation and getting a charge out of each one of those things I truly figured I could never appreciate again. In May 2015, after just finishing a 10K, I applied to run the London Marathon for St George's and Queen Mary's Hospital foundations to attempt to collect some cash and give a minor piece back in contrast with what they gave me — my life. I got acknowledged in October 2015 and finished the London Marathon 2016 (3 years sooner than foreseen) while raising a huge £14,000 for the philanthropy.

Since that day in 2014 I have drawn in to my accomplice who stood solidly close by through every last bit of it, came back to uni and completed my degree (something I never figured I would), came back to work, ran the long distance race, been on 3 occasions and I have reestablished enthusiasm forever and a craving to live it without limit. I have 3 additional long distance races on my rundown just as a couple skydive. Indeed, I have some awful scars. Will I ever approve of uncovering them? Most likely not. Do they trouble me? Truly they do, I'd lie on the off chance that I said they didn't, however the truth is those scars recount to a story – a story that says 'I endure', 'I was more grounded than whatever attempted to break me' since I'm still here.

Regardless i'm grinning. I'm resolved to take each constructive I can out of it... my mishap has formed and welded the individual that I am today. I constantly used to state 'everything occurs for an explanation' – we may not generally realize that reason straight away and some of the time it can take years, however whether beneficial things occur or terrible things happen I accept they happen to put you on the way you should be on.

On second April 2014, my entire world was flipped around, never to be the equivalent again. It's been a physical, mental and passionate rollercoaster however what makes a difference is that I gotten the opportunity to modify it – greater, better, more joyful and more grounded than at any other time. Whatever I do now, I do with my entire being and I'm more decided than any time in recent memory to snatch what I deeply desire with two hands (and feet!) since I genuinely think the sky is the limit in the event that you simply accept. I trust that by sharing my story I can give at any rate one individual who is feeling as powerless as I once might have been, the expectation they have to get ridden at the earliest.

Campbell and Lucy's story

To begin from the earliest starting point, our story began 8 years prior where we met as two youthful, carefree Club 18-30 reps. One from Essex, one from (the opulent piece of) Glasgow. Who would've thought 6 years after the fact, we would even now be as one and I would state "yes" to Campbell who was bowing down before me on one knee before my entire family (despite everything I can't accept he did that!). What's more, only 3 weeks after that minute, would be the night that completely changed us.

Campbell had wanted to go for a few beverages with his work associates on Friday 28th June 2013. A couple transformed into a couple (we've all been there) and long story short, predominantly on the grounds that I don't have the foggiest idea what really occurred, Campbell fell 25 feet in the City of London landing first to his left side knee and afterward on his head.

I just scratched a C in Science, so please pardon the absence of medicinal wording, however Campbell essentially broke the left half of his face, destroyed his left knee top, was in a trance like state and goodness definitely, clearly continued a Traumatic Brain Injury. Anybody that has experienced this, when you hear the words "cerebrum damage" referenced, it is practically at that phase that your reality self-destructs. Be that as it may, saying that, I was as yet persuaded that I would take Campbell home from clinic in two or three days! How innocent I was!

Campbell was in a trance like state for around 3 weeks. In any event I think it was, despite everything I thought he was in a state of extreme lethargy around 2 months a short time later however was informed that he had left that various weeks back! I think the entire stun of everything marginally slanted my insight.

He was at the Royal London (who were splendid coincidentally) at first for the initial 3 months, at that point got a spot at the Regional Rehabilitation Unit at Northwick Park Hospital for a half year.

At the point when I think back now, I truly don't have the foggiest idea how I endured this a half year. Campbell was truly not well overall. He was in the "Low State of Awareness" organize now, I think they call it "developing".

What this implies in ordinary terms is that Campbell couldn't talk, walk, eat, go to the latrine for himself and evidently had transformed into an irate, harsh and forceful individual that I didn't perceive. That was probably the hardest thing to manage I think. I forgot about the measure of times I was sorry to the staff at the RRU for things that Campbell had said to them. I continually ended up saying "I guarantee he wasn't care for that previously". The staff know as this is so basic with his kind of damage however regardless you believe you have to protect them!

At the purpose of Campbell leaving Northwick Park he was at long last starting to gain ground (it wasn't solid for some time). His next stop was at a concentrated recovery unit called Blackheath Brain Injury Rehabilitation Unit.

In addition to the fact that this was a decent situation for him, yet it was likewise nearer to me. Upminster to Northwick Park is certainly not a pleasant adventure each day, especially when you are working all day (how could I do it?!).

Blackheath did something amazing for Campbell and he soon figured out how to walk and eat for himself and was improving constantly, with the assistance of the specialists. It was here that he was permitted his first excursion out to Greenwich Park. It endured around 10 minutes because of his capacity to focus and I am almost certain he blew up at a couple of pigeons however it was the best 10 minutes of my life. The outrage and damaging conduct was still there at

Blackheath and memory and perception were unquestionably still his primary issues however he was making enhancements in these zones.

Following 7 months at Blackheath and a great deal of diligent work, the following stop was Marillac. This is a moderate stream unit situated in Brentwood, Essex and above all, just around a brief drive from my home! Campbell landed there on seventeenth July 2014 (day after my 30th birthday celebration) and this is the place he will remain until he in the long run gets back home. Treatment sessions are colossally decreased here yet the fundamental positive is that Campbell gets the chance to return home for supper consistently and as of late he has been getting back home to remain for quite a long time.

Try not to misunderstand me, it isn't all plain cruising, regardless he has forceful upheavals (chiefly at my "hefty feline") and I swear he thinks I am a mobile reference book with the measure of inquiries he pose to me. His memory is frequently a test also and he asks me similar inquiries around 300 times each week. That might be a slight misrepresentation. All that is justified, despite all the trouble however, for even 5 minutes of having him at home once more.

Regardless we have far to go despite everything I have a few objectives that I need Campbell to accomplish, the fundamental one being getting him back to some type of business. The primary issue right now is his absence of understanding into his damage which is the essential reason to some of his issues right now. I will get him there, trust me when I state that!

The primary concern that I can say that has got me through this, be it through family, companions, advisors and Headway, is an encouraging group of people. I unquestionably couldn't have done this without everybody supporting me.

I don't think it is conceivable to depict what the previous year and half has been similar to. I think my feelings have extended from blame, outrage, self indulgence and desire to give some examples. Be that as it may, most importantly, the most significant thing is that I kept my comical inclination, regardless I carried on with my life by guaranteeing despite everything I went out and let my hair down with my stunning gathering of companions and I ensured that I focussed on my work so as long as I can remember wasn't just about Campbell. I do likewise imagine that the Marlborough locale of New Zealand has had an enormous elevate in benefits in their Sauvingnon Blanc following Campbell's mishap!

Campbell will get back home in the New Year where the arrangement will be for us to ideally move into our home, which was intended to be the arrangement a year ago. It will be intense yet I am as yet fortunate that he is here, though with a couple of increments to the old Campbell that I knew.

Expedite our wedding, I am speculating there might be a couple of tears.

Christopher's story

I still right up 'til the present time can't recollect the first occasion when I woke up in ICU (Intensive Care Unit). On the off chance that you ask me what my first particular memory was after I woke up, it would bring me a further month down the line to what I presently observe to be a rousing get up and go talk from the ward nurture. It included an exacting berating about kicking up on the off chance that I needed to be out of medical clinic before Christmas. I went through a quarter of a year behind the dividers of the (old) Royal London Hospital, three weeks of which were spent in an initiated trance like state and a further month with debilitated cognizance from the prescription I was on. Be that as it may, how could I arrive?

To consider me a sharp cyclist would have been putting it mildly. Cycling was my life, an energy which developed from the test, accommodation and endorphin surge that it gave me. My motivation for going out for a cycle on the 22nd June 2010 is as yet vague and my recollections of that morning stay dim. I do review the London Bikeathon being close, an occasion I had entered in my offered to collect some cash for the Lymphoma and

Leukemia malignant growth philanthropy. So normally I accept I was blaming this last cycle so as to keep preparing.

I had made it to the extent the Cross Way Boulevard, a ring street that flows Bluewater strip mall, when unexpectedly I was having that very get up and go chat with this attendant. Long stretches of my life disappeared at the flicker of an eye. I had been engaged with a cycling street traffic episode. While accelerating along a carriageway on my two wheeled steed, a vehicle in overabundance of 50mph had lost control from behind and tossed me 30ft into the following path, just for me to then be centimeters from a second impact from an after vehicle. I was without a doubt in an awful shape and it had taken two months in medical clinic to at long last settle and get a genuine valuation for my wounds.

My prompt danger was the interior dying. Witness proclamations recommended I reacted at the location of the mishap, just to sit up and breakdown through a huge measure of blood misfortune and the supported head damage. The Kent Air Ambulance flew out to my guide and I was anesthetized on scene to control the agony and side effects of growing. I required 96 pints of blood throughout the following 48 hours of my recuperation. A procedure I have just the blood donators to thank. The blood misfortune came because of different outside and inside cuts. Among the numerous I envision it was the 14 to 16 inch cut over my lower back that prompted 12 minutes of heart failure. An injury whose scar is one of endless that go about as steady tokens of my difficulty.

The principal activity was to balance out my body and was one of ordinarily that my folks were approached to say goodbye to me. I was not expected to endure this activity and by shy of a marvel I have the delight of composing this today.

The following activity was trying to fix my spine. The effect from the vehicle had cracked and broken three vertebrae in the Lumbar and Thoracic areas. Metal bars and sticks were embedded to help and help the recuperating of bone. They were embedded with such exactness and aptitude that I can be appreciative for the fruitful fix, yet in addition for the fragile entry point imprints made to my skin through the miracles of keyhole medical procedure. In any case, this didn't make versatility any simpler and was additionally compounded still by the two noteworthy cracks to my pelvis.

Physiotherapy would have been a battle and it was a scaffold I was far from intersection.

Having metal in your back is not all that much, yet it was constantly a decent friendly exchange. I expected it would be in there until I (authoritatively) kicked the pail but then incredibly it just kept going about a year. The minute I discovered that I had broken the spinal metalwork ought to never have truly been a shock, given I began to feel a crunching sensation underneath the skin at whatever point I would wind my back. Regardless of the reality of this circumstance, the manner in which this data was broken to me was cheerful at its absolute best. After going for a crisis X-beam, the specialist turned out to the holding up zone and tended to me with the accompanying words:

"Mr Woodhams? [yes] Do you realize you have metal in your back?"

Envision his response on the off chance that I had said no?

"Well it is broken". Not exactly the news I needed to hear. Safe to state it wasn't some time before I was back in the working theater and the metal was expelled.

Of the considerable number of wounds it was the head that represented the best of concerns, and which is all well and good, for it was going to direct the personal satisfaction I was to lead. Regardless of whether I was to endure, the inquiry still waited with respect to whether I would have the option to talk, have an independent perspective and carry on with the ordinary life I recently had.

The chances were against me if you somehow managed to consider that I had been unconscious for three weeks. Two hours preceding arousing my folks and family were cautioned that on the off chance that I at any point woke up from my trance like state they could expect my loss of motion starting from the waist and that I may never again remember them. By a long shot shy of another wonder, my dad and auntie saw the primary promising indications of life. I jerked my foot in light of an order and perceived a 90's work of art, 'Drive it' by 'Salt-n-Pepa' that my dad was murmuring; I was wakeful.

Similarly as with any recuperation progress, there will be the 'high points and low points'. Exactly when my family members and restorative staff had any expectation of my soundness and had taken me off different anti-infection agents, my wellbeing plunged. I was currently obscuring my discourse and tearing my cannulas out in my insane state. Plainly something had turned out badly. Restorative staff quick pointed the finger towards my head damage, yet my family were not tolerating this. Further tests immediately distinguished the reason to be my left Gluteus Maximus having gone septic. My body was harming itself from within.

Prompt medical procedure spared my leg and my life, however my abandoned base cheek fell. It took 48 hours of dialysis and the correct portion of anti-infection agents to return me on the move to recuperation once more. Among the interior harms, one specifically had sneaked past the net. Giving the conditions of my condition I can't accuse restorative staff for carelessness. The effect of the vehicle had cracked my bladder neck and as to cite my specialist, my bladder was therefore "pissing out everywhere". By and by I had wound up with another poison compromising my body.

It was this very damage still makes issues this day. I am 24 at the hour of composing this (20 at the hour of the mishap) and experience the ill effects of Stress Urinary Incontinence; I wet myself during the day with debilitated urinary control. I currently carry on with an actual existence in danger from potential humiliation and a pee sack joined to my leg. It is a long way from noble and I must be cautious about what I take part in, however at any rate I am alive.

I remember my good fortune and owe an incredible obligation of appreciation to the National Health Service, the Kent Air Ambulance, physiotherapists, region medical attendants, loved ones for getting me in a good place again. If not for this talented pack I could have been in a far more awful position that what I am currently.

Incontinence is a torment, however it is such a little cost to pay.

Do I lament going out cycling that day? Obviously not. I was accomplishing something I cherished and was just in an unlucky spot. In the event that there is any message I can pass on from my mishap it would be not to underestimate life and I would pass my recently discovered understanding that none of us are strong. I succumbed to a bogus discernment that I was, and now I possibly have an unpleasant restorative life ahead. This doesn't mean I won't have a ball and make every moment count, yet it has opened my eyes to the perils and acknowledgment that occasionally the dangers we as a whole may all come to face are once in a while best stayed away from.

In the event that you ever end up in such a situation as mine, my recommendation is to keep solid disapproved, decided and set yourself objectives. I genuinely accept that even with the help and restorative aptitude that one may get, it is inspiration and fearlessness that will get your life, or if nothing else its majority, back once more. Fare thee well.

Definition

The Diagnostic and Statistical Manual of Mental Disorders (DSM-IV-TR) characterizes injury as immediate individual experience of an occasion that includes genuine or compromised demise or genuine damage; danger to one's physical respectability, seeing an occasion that includes the above experience, finding out about unforeseen or brutal passing, genuine mischief, or risk of death, or damage experienced by a relative or close partner. Recollections related with injury are ordinarily unequivocal, sound, and hard to forget. The individual's reaction to aversive subtleties of awful accident include exceptional dread, powerlessness or repulsiveness. In youngsters it is showed as disarranged or agitative behaviors.

Injury can be brought about by a wide assortment of occasions, however there are a couple of normal perspectives. There is every now and again an infringement of the individual's center suppositions about the world and their human rights, placing the individual in a condition of extraordinary disarray and weakness. This is seen when organizations relied on for endurance abuse, mortify, double-cross, or cause significant misfortunes or detachments as opposed to summoning viewpoints like constructive self-esteem, safe limits and individual freedom.

Mentally horrible encounters regularly include physical injury that compromises one's endurance and feeling of security. Typical causes and risks of mental injury incorporate badgering, shame, deserting, damaging connections, dismissal, codependence, physical ambush, sexual misuse, accomplice battery, business segregation, police fierceness, legal defilement and offense, harassing, paternalism, aggressive behavior at home, teaching, being the casualty of a heavy drinker parent, the danger or the seeing of savagery (especially in youth), hazardous ailments, and drug incited trauma. Catastrophic cataclysmic events, for example, seismic tremors and volcanic ejections, huge scale transportation mishaps, house or local fire, engine vehicle mishap, mass relational brutality like war, fear based oppressor assaults or different mass exploitation like sex dealing, being taken as a prisoner or being abducted can likewise cause mental injury. Long haul presentation to circumstances, for example, outrageous destitution or different types of misuse, for example, obnoxious attack, exist autonomously of physical injury yet at the same time produce mental injury.

Reacting to trauma

Keep in mind that numerous progressions after an injury are ordinary. Indeed, a great many people who straightforwardly experience an awful mishap have serious issues in the quick repercussions. Numerous individuals at that point feel greatly improved inside 3 months after the occasion, however others recuperate all the more gradually, and some keep on encountering incapacitating indications. The initial move toward recuperation is getting progressively mindful of the progressions that you have experienced since the injury. The absolute most regular issues after an injury incorporate the accompanying.

1. Uneasiness and dread. Nervousness is a typical and common reaction to a risky circumstance. For some individuals it keeps going long after the injury finished. This happens when perspectives on the world and a feeling of security have changed. You may become on edge when you recollect the injury. Be that as it may, here and there tension may originate from all of a sudden. Triggers or prompts that can cause uneasiness may incorporate spots, times of day, certain scents or commotions, or any circumstance that helps you to remember the injury. As you give more consideration to the occasions when you feel on edge, you can find the triggers for your uneasiness. Along these lines, you may discover that a portion of the out of nowhere uneasiness is truly activated by things that help you to remember your injury.

2. Re-encountering of the injury. Individuals frequently "re-experience" the awful mishap. For instance, you may have undesirable contemplations of the injury and get yourself incapable to dispose of them. A few people have flashbacks, or very striking pictures, which can feel as though the injury is happening once more. Bad dreams are likewise normal. These side effects happen in light of the fact that a horrendous encounter is so stunning thus not the same as ordinary encounters that you can't fit it into what you think about the world. So as to comprehend what occurred, your mind holds bringing the memory back, as though to all the more likely summary it and fit it in with your encounters.

3. Expanded cautiousness is likewise a typical reaction to injury. This incorporates feeling "on monitor," anxious, unsteady, flimsy, apprehensive, tense, being effectively surprised, and experiencing difficulty focusing

or dozing. Ceaseless watchfulness can prompt anxiety and touchiness, particularly in case you're not getting enough rest. This response is because of the stop (e.g., deer in the headlights), battle or escape reaction in your body, and is simply the manner in which we secure against peril. Creatures likewise have the stop, battle or escape reaction when looked with risk. At the point when we shield ourselves from genuine threat by solidifying, battling or escaping, we need significantly more vitality than expected, so our bodies siphon out additional adrenaline to assist us with getting the additional vitality we have to endure.

(p. 139) People who have encountered a horrible mishap may consider the to be as loaded up with risk, so their bodies are on steady alert, constantly prepared to react promptly to any assault. The issue is that expanded carefulness is helpful in really hazardous circumstances, for example, on the off chance that you are in a combat area or you are being looted. Be that as it may, expanded watchfulness gets destructive, when it proceeds for quite a while even in safe circumstances.

4. Evasion is a typical method for attempting to oversee PTSD indications. The most widely recognized is staying away from circumstances that help you to remember the injury, for example, where it occurred. Regularly, circumstances that are less straightforwardly identified with the injury are likewise kept away from, for example, going out at night if the injury happened around evening time, or going to swarmed regions, for example, the market, shopping center or cinema.

Another basic evasion strategy is to attempt to push away excruciating considerations and emotions. This can prompt sentiments of deadness or vacancy, where you think that its hard to feel any feelings, even positive ones. Now and then the excruciating contemplations or emotions might be exceptional to the point that your mind just squares them out through and through, and you may not recall portions of the injury.

5. Numerous individuals who have encountered an awful accident feel irate. On the off chance that you are not used to feeling furious, this may appear to be frightening also. It might be particularly befuddling to feel furious at the individuals who are nearest to you. Individuals now and then go to substances to attempt to lessen these sentiments of outrage.

6. Injury may prompt sentiments of blame and disgrace. Numerous individuals censure themselves for things they did or didn't do to endure. For instance, some ambush survivors accept that they ought to have fended off an attacker, and reprimand themselves for the assault. Other people who may have endure an occasion wherein others died feel that they ought to have been the one to bite the dust, or that they ought to have had the option to by one way or another keep the other individual from kicking the bucket. In some cases, other individuals may censure you for the injury.

Feeling remorseful about the injury implies that you are assuming liability for what happened. At the same time may make you feel to some degree more in charge, it is normally uneven, off base and can prompt sentiments of discouragement.

7. Pain and gloom are likewise basic responses to injury. This can incorporate inclination down, miserable, or sad. You may cry all the more regularly. You may lose enthusiasm for individuals and exercises that you used to appreciate. You may remain at home and detach yourself from companions. You may likewise feel that plans you had for the future don't appear to make a difference any longer, or that life does not merit living. These emotions can prompt considerations of wanting to be dead, or planning something for attempt to damage or execute yourself. Since the injury has changed such a large amount of how you see the world and yourself, it bodes well to feel pitiful and to lament for what you lost as a result of the awful experience. In the event that you have these sentiments or considerations, it is significant that you converse with your (p. 140) specialist. Your specialist is prepared in

95

how to deal with these musings and encounters and will assist you with overcoming this.

8. Mental self view and perspectives on the world regularly become progressively negative after an injury. You may let yourself know, "On the off chance that I wasn't so feeble this wouldn't have transpired." Many individuals see themselves in a progressively contrary light by and large after the injury ("I am an awful individual and I merited this").

It is likewise extremely normal to see others all the more contrarily, and to feel that you can't confide in anybody. On the off chance that you used to consider the world as a sheltered spot, the injury may abruptly make you imagine that the world is exceptionally hazardous. In the event that you had past terrible encounters, the injury may persuade you that the world is for sure hazardous and others are not to be trusted. These antagonistic musings frequently make individuals feel they have been changed totally by the injury. Associations with others can get tense, and closeness turns out to be increasingly troublesome as your trust diminishes.

9. Sexual connections may likewise endure after a horrendous encounter. Numerous individuals think that its hard to feel cozy or to have sexual connections once more. This is particularly valid for the individuals who have been explicitly attacked, since notwithstanding the absence of trust, sex itself can be a token of the ambush.

10. Numerous individuals increment their utilization of liquor or different substances after an injury. Regularly, they do this trying

to "self-cure" or to shut out agonizing recollections, considerations, or sentiments identified with the injury. Individuals with PTSD may experience difficulty resting or may have bad dreams, and they may utilize liquor or medications to attempt to improve rest or not recall their fantasies. While it might appear to help temporarily, interminable utilization of liquor or medications will back off (or anticipate) your recuperation from PTSD and will cause issues of its own. Luckily, there are medications, for example, this one, that can assist you with recuperating from PTSD and experience long haul help from indications without the utilization of liquor or medications.

Acute stress disorder

ASD is a generally new mental determination. The American Psychiatric Association previously acquainted it with the fourth release of the Diagnostic and Statistical Manual of Mental Health Disorders in 1994.

In spite of the fact that it shares huge numbers of indistinguishable manifestations from PTSD, ASD is a particular determination. An individual with ASD encounters mental trouble promptly following a horrendous mishap. In contrast to PTSD, ASD is a brief condition, and side effects normally persevere for at any rate 3 to 30 days after the horrible accident. In the event that an individual encounters side effects for longer than a month, a specialist will generally evaluate them for PTSD.

Side effects

Individuals who have ASD experience side effects like those of PTSD and different pressure issue.

ASD manifestations fall under five general categories

Interruption manifestations. These happen when an individual can't quit returning to a horrible accident through flashbacks, recollections, or dreams.

Negative mind-set. An individual may experience negative musings, trouble, and low state of mind.

Dissociative indications. These can incorporate an adjusted feeling of the real world, an absence of consciousness of the environment, and a powerlessness to recollect portions of the horrendous mishap.

Evasion indications. Individuals with these side effects deliberately keep away from considerations, sentiments, individuals, or spots that they partner with the horrible mishap.

Excitement indications. These can incorporate a sleeping disorder and other rest unsettling influences, trouble concentrating, and crabbiness or animosity, which can be either verbal or physical. The individual may likewise feel tense or on watchman and become alarmed effectively.

Individuals with ASD may build up extra emotional wellness issue, for example, uneasiness and wretchedness.

Manifestations of nervousness include:

feeling a feeling of approaching fate

unnecessary stressing

trouble concentrating

weakness

eagerness

hustling musings

Manifestations of wretchedness include:

tireless sentiments of misery, pity, or deadness

weakness

crying out of the blue

loss of enthusiasm for exercises that were once pleasurable

changes in craving or body weight

contemplations of suicide or self-hurt

Post-Traumatic Stress Disorder (Symptoms and Different Types of PTSD)

Post-awful pressure issue (PTSD) is a psychological well-being condition that is activated by a startling occasion — either encountering it or seeing it. Indications may incorporate flashbacks, bad dreams and serious nervousness, just as wild musings about the occasion.

The vast majority who experience awful mishaps may have transitory trouble altering and adapting, yet with time and great self-care, they generally show signs of improvement. In the event that the manifestations deteriorate, keep going for quite a long time or even years, and meddle with your everyday working, you may have PTSD.

Getting viable treatment after PTSD side effects create can be basic to diminish side effects and improve work.

Items and Services

Bulletin: Mayo Clinic Health Letter

Indications

Post-horrible pressure issue manifestations may begin inside one month of a horrendous mishap, however some of the time indications may not show up until years after the occasion. These side effects cause noteworthy issues in social or work circumstances and seeing someone. They can likewise meddle with your capacity to approach your ordinary every day errands.

PTSD indications are commonly gathered into four kinds: meddlesome recollections, evasion, negative changes in speculation and mind-set, and changes in physical and passionate responses. Indications can shift after some time or differ from individual to individual.

Nosy recollections

Manifestations of meddlesome recollections may include:

Intermittent, undesirable troubling recollections of the awful accident

Remembering the horrible accident as though it were going on once more (flashbacks)

Upsetting dreams or bad dreams about the horrible accident

Serious enthusiastic trouble or physical responses to something that helps you to remember the awful accident

Shirking

Indications of evasion may include:

Attempting to abstain from pondering the awful mishap

Keeping away from spots, exercises or individuals that help you to remember the horrible mishap

Negative changes in deduction and state of mind

Manifestations of negative changes in intuition and state of mind may include:

Contrary contemplations about yourself, other individuals or the world

Misery about what's to come

Memory issues, including not recalling significant parts of the horrible mishap

Trouble keeping up cozy connections

Feeling separated from loved ones

Absence of enthusiasm for exercises you once delighted in

Trouble encountering positive feelings

Feeling sincerely numb

Changes in physical and passionate responses

Indications of changes in physical and passionate responses (additionally called excitement manifestations) may include:

Being effectively surprised or scared

Continually being wary for threat

Reckless conduct, for example, drinking excessively or driving also quick

Issue dozing

Issue concentrating

Fractiousness, furious upheavals or forceful conduct

Overpowering blame or disgrace

For youngsters 6 years of age and more youthful, signs and manifestations may likewise include:

Re-ordering the awful mishap or parts of the horrendous accident through play

Terrifying dreams that might possibly incorporate parts of the horrible accident

Force of side effects

PTSD indications can differ in force after some time. You may have more PTSD side effects when you're worried all in all, or when you run over tokens of what you experienced. For instance, you may hear a vehicle reverse discharge and remember battle encounters. Or on the other hand you may see a report on the report about a rape and feel defeat by recollections of your own attack.

When to see a specialist

On the off chance that you have upsetting considerations and emotions about a horrible accident for over a month, on the off chance that they're extreme, or on the off chance that you feel you're experiencing difficulty recovering your life leveled out, converse with your primary care physician or a psychological wellness proficient. Getting treatment as quickly as time permits can help keep PTSD indications from deteriorating.

In the event that you have self-destructive musings

In the event that you or somebody you know has self-destructive musings, get help immediately through at least one of these assets:

Connect with a dear companion or adored one.

Contact a pastor, a profound pioneer or somebody in your confidence network.

Call a suicide hotline number — in the United States, call the National Suicide Prevention Lifeline at 1-800-273-TALK (1-800-273-8255) to arrive at a prepared advisor. Utilize that equivalent number and press 1 to arrive at the Veterans Crisis Line.

Make a meeting with your primary care physician or a psychological wellness proficient.

When to get crisis help

In the event that you figure you may hurt yourself or endeavor suicide, call 911 or your nearby crisis number right away.

On the off chance that you realize somebody who's in peril of endeavoring suicide or has made a suicide endeavor, ensure somebody remains with that individual to keep the person in question safe. Call 911 or your nearby crisis number right away. Or on the other hand, in the event that you can do so securely, take the individual to the closest clinic crisis room.

Remembering Trauma

Our recollections are not ideal reproductions of the past. Rather, recollecting a past occasion is a mix of procedures, sorting out many separate subtleties, and making surmisings to fill in the holes to make an intelligible entirety. Typically, these inferential procedures work well for us, enabling us to settle on quick and precise choices about what we've seen and done. Be that as it may, no framework dependent on inductions will be 100% precise.

Our present drives, inclinations, generalizations, and desires would all be able to influence that inferential procedure, in a general sense twisting what we 'recall.' While it may be anything but difficult to acknowledge that our recollections for commonplace encounters can be contorted in such a manner, individuals have since quite a while ago clung to the idea that horrendous recollections are extraordinary, that they are shielded from any sort of memory mutilation.

Actually, combining proof exhibits that encounters of injury, regardless of whether a solitary occasion (e.g., a rape) or a continued unpleasant encounter that may include various injury types (e.g., encounters at war) are additionally helpless against memory twisting. Truth be told, horrible memory twisting seems to pursue a specific example: individuals will in general experienced considerably more injury than they really did. This normally converts into more noteworthy seriousness of Post-horrible Stress Disorder (PTSD) indications after some time, as the recalled injury "develops." (For research articles archiving this, see the references refered to in this post.)

Open Domain

Basically, over-recollecting injury as a rule prompts more unfortunate emotional well-being results. In one model, Southwick et al. asked Desert Storm veterans at multi month and 2 years after their arrival from administration, regardless of whether certain occasions happened during that administration (e.g., encountering rifleman discharge, sitting with a withering partner). They discovered 88% of veterans changed their reaction to in any event one occasion and 61% changed mutiple. Significantly, most of those progressions were from "no, that didn't transpire" to "indeed, that transpired." as anyone might expect, this 'over-recalling' was related with an expansion in PTSD manifestations.

For what reason would this be? From a transformative viewpoint, it would not appear to be versatile to recall an occasion as progressively horrible after some time; that would expand passionate torment and the devastating indications of PTSD, in this way postponing recuperation.

One potential clarification is that, while the mistakes themselves are not versatile, they are an unavoidable result of a generally ground-breaking and adaptable memory framework. This is similar to the human ACL: in spite of the fact that it is a shaky area in our knees, it is a result of a generally positive adjustment: bipedalism. It might be that over-recollecting injury—simply like different sorts of memory blunders—are the consequence of a disappointment in something many refer to as the source checking process.

Quickly, as per the Source Monitoring Framework, individuals don't store the subtleties of an involvement in their memory joined by names indicating their birthplaces. Rather, they depend on heuristics, for example, how recognizable the occasion subtleties feel, to decide if a recollected detail really happened or was simply proposed or envisioned. Basically, post-occasion handling, for example, effectively envisioning new subtleties or encountering undesirable meddlesome musings—can build the recognition of new subtleties enough that individuals may erroneously guarantee those new subtleties as certified memory follows. This is memory bending.

Feeling Safe

Passionate and mental injury is the consequence of phenomenally upsetting occasions that break your suspicion that all is well and good, making you feel defenseless in a risky world. Horrible encounters regularly include a risk to life or wellbeing, yet any circumstance that leaves you feeling overpowered and disconnected can bring about injury, regardless of whether it doesn't include physical hurt. It's not the target conditions that decide if an occasion is horrible, however your abstract passionate experience of the occasion. The more terrified and defenseless you feel, the almost certain you are to be damaged.

Passionate and mental injury can be brought about by:

Once occasions, for example, mishap, damage, or a savage assault, particularly on the off chance that it was surprising or occurred in youth. Progressing, tenacious pressure, for example, living in a wrongdoing ridden neighborhood, fighting a hazardous disease or encountering horrendous accidents that happen over and again, for example, tormenting, abusive behavior at home, or youth disregard.

Usually ignored causes, for example, medical procedure (particularly in the initial 3 years of life), the unexpected passing of somebody close, the separation of a critical relationship, or a mortifying or profoundly baffling background, particularly on the off chance that somebody was intentionally unfeeling.

Adapting to the injury of a characteristic or synthetic fiasco can show exceptional difficulties—regardless of whether you weren't straightforwardly associated with the occasion. Truth be told, while it's profoundly far-fetched any of us will ever be the immediate casualties of a psychological militant assault, plane accident, or mass shooting, for instance, we're all routinely shelled by terrible pictures via web-based networking media and news wellsprings of those individuals who have been. Review these pictures again and again can overpower your sensory system and make horrendous pressure.

Youth injury and the danger of future injury

While horrendous accidents can transpire, you're bound to be damaged by an occasion in case you're as of now under an overwhelming pressure load, have as of late endured a progression of misfortunes, or have been damaged previously—particularly if the prior injury happened in youth. Youth injury can come about because of anything that upsets a youngster's feeling of security, including:

A flimsy or hazardous condition

Partition from a parent

Genuine sickness

Meddling restorative techniques

Sexual, physical, or boisterous attack

Aggressive behavior at home

Disregard

Encountering injury in adolescence can bring about an extreme and durable impact. At the point when youth injury isn't settled, a feeling of dread and defenselessness continues into adulthood, making way for further injury. Notwithstanding, regardless of whether your injury happened numerous years back, there are steps you can take to beat the agony, figure out how to trust and interface with others once more, and recover your feeling of enthusiastic equalization.

Side effects of mental injury

We as a whole respond to injury in various manners, encountering a wide scope of physical and passionate responses. There is no "right" or "wrong" approach to think, feel, or react, so don't pass judgment on your own responses or those of other individuals. Your reactions are NORMAL responses to ABNORMAL occasions.

Passionate and mental indications:

Stun, forswearing, or mistrust

Disarray, trouble concentrating

Outrage, touchiness, state of mind swings

Tension and dread

Blame, disgrace, self-fault

Pulling back from others

Feeling miserable or sad

Feeling detached or numb

Physical side effects:

A sleeping disorder or bad dreams

Weariness

Being alarmed effectively

Trouble concentrating

Dashing heartbeat

Tenseness and fomentation

A throbbing painfulness

Muscle pressure

Mending from injury

Injury side effects regularly last from a couple of days to a couple of months, step by step blurring as you process the disrupting occasion. Be that as it may, in any event, when you're feeling much improved, you might be beset every once in a while by excruciating recollections or feelings— particularly in light of triggers, for example, a commemoration of the occasion or something that helps you to remember the injury. On the off chance that your mental injury manifestations don't simplicity up—or on the off chance that they become much more terrible—and you find that you can't proceed onward from the occasion for a drawn out timeframe, you might be encountering Post-Traumatic Stress Disorder (PTSD). While enthusiastic injury is an ordinary reaction to an upsetting occasion, it becomes PTSD when your sensory system gets "stuck" and you stay in mental stun, unfit to comprehend what occurred or procedure your feelings.

Regardless of whether a horrible accident includes passing, you as a survivor must adapt to the misfortune, at any rate incidentally, of your feeling of wellbeing. The normal response to this misfortune is despondency. Like individuals who have lost a friend or family member, you have to experience a lamenting procedure. The accompanying tips can assist you with adapting to the feeling of sadness, mend from the injury, and proceed onward with your life.

Injury recuperation tip 1: Get moving

Injury upsets your body's common harmony, solidifying you in a condition of hyperarousal and dread. Just as consuming off adrenaline and discharging endorphins, exercise and development can really help fix your sensory system. Attempt to practice for 30 minutes or more on generally days. Or on the other hand if it's simpler, three 10-minute spurts of activity every day are similarly as great. Exercise that is cadenced and draws in both your arms and legs, for example, strolling, running, swimming, ball, or in any event, moving—works best. Include a care component. Rather than concentrating on your considerations or diverting yourself while you work out, truly center around your body and how it feels as you move. Notice the vibe of your feet hitting the ground, for instance, or the musicality of your breathing, or the sentiment of wind on your skin. Shake climbing, boxing, weight preparing, or hand to hand fighting can make this simpler—all things considered, you have to concentrate on your body developments during these exercises so as to stay away from damage.

Tip 2: Don't disconnect

Following an injury, you might need to pull back from others, however disconnection just compounds the situation. Interfacing with others eye to eye will enable you to recuperate, so attempt to keep up your connections and abstain from investing an excess of energy alone. You don't need to discuss the injury. Interfacing with others doesn't need to include discussing the injury. Truth be told, for certain individuals, that can simply compound the situation. Solace originates from feeling connected with and acknowledged by others.

Request support. While you don't need to discuss the injury itself, it is significant that you have somebody to impart your emotions to eye to eye, somebody who will listen mindfully without making a decision about you. Go to a confided in relative, companion, instructor, or minister.

Partake in social exercises, regardless of whether you don't feel like it. Do "typical" exercises with other individuals, exercises that have nothing to do with the horrendous experience.

Reconnect with old companions. On the off chance that you've withdrawn from connections that were once imperative to you, attempt to reconnect. Join a care group for injury survivors. Associating with other people who are confronting similar issues can help lessen your feeling of seclusion, and hearing how others adapt can help motivate you in your own recuperation. Volunteer. Just as helping other people, volunteering can be an extraordinary method to challenge the feeling of vulnerability that regularly goes with injury. Help yourself to remember your qualities and recover your feeling of intensity by helping other people. Make new companions. On the off chance that you live alone or a long way from loved ones, it's essential to connect and make new companions. Take a class or join a club to meet individuals with comparative interests, interface with a graduated class affiliation, or connect with neighbors or work associates. In the event that interfacing with others is troublesome

Numerous individuals who have encountered injury feel detached, pulled back and think that its hard to interface with other individuals. In the event that that depicts you, there are a few moves you can make before you next meet with a companion: Exercise or move. Bounce all over, swing your arms and legs, or simply thrash around. Your head will feel more clear and you'll see it simpler to interface. Vocal conditioning. As abnormal as it sounds, vocal conditioning is an extraordinary method to open up to social commitment. Sit upright and just make "mmmm" sounds. Change the pitch and volume until you experience a charming vibration in your face.

Tip 3: Self-manage your sensory system

Regardless of how fomented, on edge, or crazy you feel, realize that you can change your excitement framework and quiet yourself. Not exclusively will it help mitigate the uneasiness related with injury, however it will likewise cause a more noteworthy feeling of control. Careful relaxing. On the off chance that you are feeling muddled, befuddled, or upset, rehearsing careful breathing is a fast method to quiet yourself. Basically take 60 breaths, concentrating on each 'out' breath. Tangible input. Does a particular sight, smell or taste rapidly make you feel quiet? Or then again perhaps petting a creature or tuning in to music attempts to rapidly alleviate you? Everybody reacts to tactile information somewhat better, so try different things with various speedy pressure alleviation strategies to discover what works best for you. Staying grounded. To feel in the present and more grounded, sit on a seat. Feel your feet on the ground and your back against the seat. Check out you and pick six items that have red or blue in them. Notice how your breathing gets further and quieter. Enable yourself to feel what you feel when you feel it. Recognize your emotions about the injury as they emerge and acknowledge them. Help Guide's Emotional Intelligence Toolkit can help.

Tip 4: Take care of your wellbeing

It's actual: having a sound body can build your capacity to adapt to the pressure of injury.

Get a lot of rest. After a horrendous encounter, stress or dread may upset your rest designs. In any case, an absence of value rest can intensify your injury manifestations and make it harder to keep up your enthusiastic parity. Rest and get up simultaneously every day and go for 7 to 9 hours of rest each night

Chapter 2 Necessary conditions before starting work

It's essential to comprehend your working environment rights and obligations with respect to pay and conditions, wellbeing and security and working environment harassing.

By law, your boss is answerable for ensuring:

your workplace is sheltered and giving suitable defensive hardware if important

laborers are free from segregation and tormenting

you get every one of your qualifications as far as pay and conditions.

As a specialist, you are answerable for:

Understanding the states of your work. This incorporates knowing your pace of pay, working hours and privileges to breaks and leave working in a way that isn't unsafe to the wellbeing and security of yourself or others comprehending what to do in the event that you think your boss isn't meeting their duties.

Ensure you:

Comprehend the states of your business. This incorporates your pace of pay, working hours and your qualifications for breaks, leave and open occasions realize your privileges concerning segregation and harassing. Realize what to do in the event that you experience or witness this in your working environment know the wellbeing and security necessities of your work environment. Ability to keep up a protected situation for yourself as well as other people approach the entirety of the fitting wellbeing apparatus and gear. Recognize what to do in case of a mishap realize where to find support on working environment wellbeing and security issues pertinent to your state or domain.

Consistently I get notification from individuals urgently attempting to become fruitful business visionaries. They unavoidably have heaps of essential inquiries that right away reveal to me they've dove in rashly and, subsequently, have seriously restricted their odds of making it all alone.

I'm certain that is not what you need to hear, however on the off chance that I don't come clean with you, at that point who will? The issue is that is the incorrect method to do it. The hands-down most ideal approach to turn into an effective business visionary is to do whatever it takes not to turn into a business visionary in any case.

Pause, what? That doesn't bode well. It seems like a logical inconsistency.

On the contrary, it makes total sense. Not just that, it's the best counsel on business you'll ever get. The thing is, no one turns into a fruitful business visionary as time goes on by embarking to get one. It happens naturally under specific conditions.

Related: 10 Behaviors of High Achievers

The issue is one of aggressive markets. Enterprise is about business, and a business that beats the challenge and takes off isn't so natural to create. For a dare to have even barely any possibility at all of making it, a few variables need to meet up:

Opportunity.

Like it or not, openings don't simply fly out of your Mac's screen and yell, "Here I am!" You need to go out and discover them and investigate them. Consider openings branches off a tree trunk. You have to get out in the genuine working world to pick up presentation to enough branches. That is the place everything else originates from.

Disclosure.

Maybe the hardest thing about a business is making sense of the correct client issue that should be illuminated. Without that, you have nothing. As a rule, that requires critical introduction, skill, and experience. Else, you'll never think of a triumphant item that beats the challenge.

Ability.

Each fruitful business visionary has a type of skill when they think of the item or organization that winds up making it. Possibly it was their obsession from the very first moment or maybe they created it while working for other people. Whichever it is, there's something they can show improvement over the pack ... and BSing isn't it.

Related: Quit Screwing Around and Get to Work

System.

Regardless of whether its value accomplices with the correct blend of ability, financial specialists, grown-up supervision, or some mix thereof, effective organizations quite often have a few key players required from the beginning or generally at an early stage. That requires a system – not an online one, a genuine system of genuine individuals you meet in reality.

Sagacious.

Not to be buzzword, yet organizations have heaps of moving parts and it is difficult to get everything cooperating except if you have a type of business insightful. There are just three spots to discover that: from your family, from business guides, or by working hands-on in the business world.

Notice that the variables cover. They're in reality all interwoven. That is the reason not embarking to turn into a business person however getting out on the planet and getting your hands grimy working is the least demanding approach to some time or another make it all alone. The genuine business world is the place each one of those conditions meet up. Furthermore, that is the place best business visionaries discover them. The main admonition is that I accept that you're searching for a type of breakout achievement where that turns into your vocation and you bring home the bacon at it. Obviously, you can slug it out with a gazillion rivals in various private companies or find success with it as a solopreneur, yet that is not actually taking the ball out of the recreation center, if you catch my drift. See, I realize this may be frustrating for some of you, however trust me when I let you know, on the off chance that you truly need to become showbiz royalty sometime in the future, you'll be ideally serviced by getting out and getting some understanding than slamming your head against a divider attempting to make sense of why things aren't working out for you.

Chapter 3 What to do to heal

Passionate injury is all over the place, thus a considerable lot of us are influenced by it.

At the point when we lose a person or thing we love, or an unpleasant occasion breaks separated our feeling that all is well with the world, we can start to see our condition and people around us as risky. Regardless of whether a specific occasion doesn't cause us any physical mischief, being in a condition of dread can in any case cause us to become damaged. Before we get into the 5 stages of mending from enthusiastic injury, we should investigate basic structures and side effects that frequently go with it.

Basic kinds of passionate injury:

• Divorce or relationship separation

• Loss of wellbeing

• Losing an employment

- Loss of budgetary security

- Miscarriage

- Retirement

- Death of a pet

- Loss of an appreciated dream

- A friend or family member's not kidding disease

- Loss of a fellowship

- Loss of security after an injury

- Selling the family home

Because of enthusiastic injury, we start to feel numb, separated and lose our trust in others. It can require some investment for this torment to leave, and for us to have a sense of security once more. On the off chance that the injury we've encountered is mental, we may experience the ill effects of disturbing recollections, uneasiness and feelings.

Injury makes a stun our brains, bodies and spirits, which can prompt passionate issues later on. There are subjective, conduct, physical, and mental responses to passionate injury.

Here are probably the most well-known passionate reactions:

• Increased excitement

• Post horrendous pressure issue

• Avoidance of social settings, companions, friends and family

• Feelings of outrage or crabbiness, sensitivity

• Sense of blame and disgrace

• Grief and discouragement

• Self-picture and perspectives on the world become progressively pessimistic

• Sexual connections endure

• Drug and liquor misuse

The passionate reactions recorded above can make us feel as if we're going insane or "losing it". Have you at any point seen that, following a horrible accident, your physical wellbeing starts to show side effects?

Regardless of whether the injury caused direct physical damage, or the substantial vitality of torment and negative feeling wore you out, the two conditions are joined by profound enthusiastic torment which can make you sick. Sleep deprivation, bad dreams, interminable exhaustion, trouble concentrating, alarm assaults, restlessness, unsettling, muscle strain and a quick heartbeat are for the most part physical side effects of passionate pressure.

Untreated passionate injury additionally has genuine symptoms.

In the event that unaddressed and left untreated, passionate injury can result in:

- Self-damaging and indiscreet practices

- Uncontrollable responsive contemplations

- Feelings of disgrace, blame, sadness, or gloom

- Loss of previous conviction frameworks

- Compulsive social issues

- Substance use difficulties

- Sexual issues

- Inability to keep up cozy connections or keep up fitting companionships

- Hostility and contentiousness

- Introversion

- Feelings of being undermined

At the point when we experience passionate injury, frequently, we're advised to concentrate on ourselves—however that can be a lot more difficult than one might expect.

At the point when it feels like the heaviness of the world is on your shoulders, it's trying to try and discover the solidarity to lift your leg, and start placing one foot before the other. Truth be told, discovering solidarity to mend from passionate injury can be absolutely debilitating and weakening now and again—notwithstanding, it's one of the most significant things you can accomplish for your prosperity. It's critical to keep up the guideline of "keeping it straightforward" when you start your recuperating venture, to maintain a strategic distance from overpower, disappointment or the craving to surrender completely. In light of that, here are five straightforward yet important strides for mending:

5 Simple Steps to Healing From Emotional Trauma

1. Be Happy to Heal

The longing to feel better can be your best partner making progress toward recuperation. Try not to yield to the self image, which will attempt to let you know there's a major issue with you: there's nothing amiss with you. The responses you experience in light of injury are just reactions—they are not what your identity is.

2. Acknowledge Support From Loved Ones

When recuperating from enthusiastic injury, it's essential to interface with others routinely and abstain from confining yourself. It takes a town to bring up a youngster, however it likewise takes a town to recuperate an individual. Encircle yourself with the individuals who backing, love and regard you will be priceless on your way to mending.

3. Look for The Assistance of Trained Professionals

You may wish to go to individual or gathering treatment, search out master feelings and get the assistance of somebody prepared in the field of passionate injury, who you feel good with and trust. Medications may concentrate on training, stress the board strategies, the arrival of body recollections, and smothered feelings that are causing physical and mental agony.

4. Practice Meditation and Mindfulness

Contemplation helps calm the jabber of the psyche, to enable you to encounter knowledge, acknowledgment and another thankfulness forever. Enthusiastic injury gets put away inside the body, so notwithstanding treatment sessions, the body extraordinarily profits by entering negligent minutes and having a care practice.

5. Fuse Movement Into Your Daily Routine

Yoga and different types of physical action discharge endorphins, and make you have a sense of security and stable. It's imperative to guarantee you consistently take part in physical action to help make positive sentiments which have been torn down from enthusiastic injury.

It might be difficult to accept this now, however you should recall the heart heals. Love yourself enough to accept that you merit shelter from agony and enduring. With confidence and ability to make the correct strides, you'll experience new degrees of delight, thankfulness, and imperativeness once you've mended.

"In the event that you are to free your heart, you should grasp your excruciating emotions, have confidence that your considerations will emerge and stop of their agreement. They will pass in the event that you can confront them head on, with kind eyes. Your musings and emotions will break up on the off chance that you don't attempt to clutch them or push them away. Thinking will scatter. Trust in this all inclusive law of progress."

– Detox Your Heart: Meditations for Healing Emotional Trauma

T – Trust yourself, family, companions and experts to help you

R – Recovery is a procedure that requires significant investment and persistence

A – Attend to yourself with affection and self-care

U – Understand enthusiastic injury isn't your flaw

M – Meditation, Mindfulness, and Movement are basic for mending

A – Accept that you are an entire individual

Chapter 4 What can help when dealing with a trauma

Fiascos and horrendous accidents can have enormous mental effects on people, regardless of whether they are not straightforwardly included. Individuals can encounter a scope of feelings, including outrage, dissatisfaction and pity, and can respond from multiple points of view, including physical and mental indications. The effects and responses can happen quickly or may show up after some time. There are steps that people can take for themselves and their families to alleviate and reduce the psychosomatic effects. This page highlights assets that can help with adapting to debacle, injury and catastrophe. After an occasion is finished, APA prescribes following these means to start adapting to the conceivable pressure that pursues a disaster:

Keep educated about new data and advancements, however stay away from overexposure to news rebroadcasts of the occasions. Make certain to utilize sound wellsprings of data to maintain a strategic distance from theory and bits of gossip.

Realize what neighborhood assets are accessible to help those influenced by the catastrophe and be set up to share this data.

On the off chance that you feel on edge, irate or discouraged, you are not the only one. Converse with companions, family or partners who likely are encountering similar sentiments.

On the off chance that you have youngsters, keep open discoursed with them in regards to their feelings of dread and the awful mishap. Tell them that in time, the catastrophe will pass. Try not to limit the risk, however talk about your capacity to adapt to disaster and get past the experience.

Sentiments of uneasiness and sorrow following an awful accident are common. On the off chance that these indications proceed, considerably after request has been reestablished, or if these sentiments start to overpower you, look for the counsel of a therapist in your locale.

Regular Reactions

Regular Reactions of Survivors of Disaster and Other Traumatic Events

Believing that nobody else is having any of similar responses and that you are distant from everyone else in managing your sentiments

Experiencing difficulty nodding off or staying unconscious

Having a feeling that you have no vitality or like you are constantly depleted

Feeling miserable or discouraged

Having stomachaches or cerebral pains

Having a feeling that you have an excessive amount of vitality or like you are hyperactive

Feeling entirely bad tempered or furious—battling with companions or family for reasons unknown

Being numb—not feeling by any stretch of the imagination

Experiencing difficulty concentrating on homework

Having times of perplexity

Drinking liquor or utilizing unlawful medications or even legitimate meds to stop your sentiments

Not having any hunger whatsoever, or the exact inverse—finding that you are eating excessively

The impacts of post-horrendous pressure issue (PTSD) can be extensive and incapacitating. The indications of PTSD can negatively affect your psychological wellness, physical wellbeing, work, and connections.

You may feel secluded, experience difficulty keeping up an occupation, be not able trust other individuals, and experience issues controlling or communicating your feelings.

Learning sound methodologies for adapting to PTSD is conceivable and can offer a feeling of restoration, expectation and command over your life. There are an assortment of territories in our lives that can be affected by the side effects of PTSD and, so as to progress in the direction of a sound recuperation, it is essential to offer regard for every region.

PTSD adapting procedures

Delineation by JR Bee, Verywell

Why Healthy Coping Skills Are Important

In the event that you have PTSD, you are at a lot more serious danger of building up various other emotional well-being issue, including uneasiness issue, misery, dietary issues, and substance use issue. For instance, analysts have discovered that individuals with PTSD are around multiple times as likely as somebody without PTSD to create sadness and around multiple times as liable to build up another nervousness disorder.1 □

Individuals with PTSD are multiple times as likely as somebody without PTSD to endeavor suicide. High paces of purposeful self-hurt have likewise been found among individuals with PTSD.

Social Coping Strategies

Attempting to disclose your experience to others can be testing. Not exclusively would it be able to be hard to chat with individuals about the horrendous mishap itself, yet it very well may be significantly all the more testing to portray to others a portion of the indications you have been encountering since the occasion.

Instruct Yourself and Others

Individuals who battle with PTSD regularly do as such in detachment, thinking that its difficult to connect. Indeed, they probably won't understand that they are battling with PTSD until the side effects become about deplorable. Notwithstanding teaching yourself on the side effects and treatment, it is imperative to search out safe individuals to associate with who can bolster you in your recuperation venture. By finding out about the condition, you can have the words to all the more obviously disclose to others what's going on for you and request what you need.

Find Supportive Connections

There are numerous assets offered in nearby networks and online that offer gathering based help, for example, bolster gatherings, classes, network gatherings, and online gatherings. Interfacing with other people who are experiencing a comparative encounter can separate the dividers of segregation and assist you with understanding that you are not the only one. Collaborating with other people who are in different phases of solid recuperation can be priceless to you in your own mending venture. You can find tips for adapting, associate with particular suppliers and find out about new and developing treatment choices.

Invest Energy With People

It is basic for individuals with PTSD to avoid individuals, pull back, and retreat.2☐ Fears, nervousness, outrage, dissatisfaction, disarray, and the sentiment of being overpowered are only a portion of the reasons why it may feel preferable to remain detached over associate with individuals.

Investing energy with strong loved ones can have a noteworthy effect in your state of mind and standpoint.

Remember that on the off chance that you are offering space to any family or companions, it is likely they as of now see you battling. Commonly individuals don't have the foggiest idea how to help or are hesitant to state something inspired by a paranoid fear of causing progressively enthusiastic agony. It tends to be useful for all gatherings—both you and your friends and family—to have the opportunity to spend together. A few different ways to invest energy with others can incorporate things like:

Taking a walk

Have morning espresso

Play a game

Chat on the telephone

Offer amusing stories

On the off chance that you don't feel prepared to talk yet, you can likewise sit discreetly in a similar space to peruse a book or the paper. Basically having a similar space unobtrusively can feel encouraging.

Discovering Social Support for Your Health and Well-Being

Passionate and Physical Coping Strategies

One of the most significant approaches to adapt to PTSD—and numerous different conditions—is to deal with your psychological and physical wellbeing. There are numerous techniques that can cooperate with your treatment to assist you with adapting to PTSD, however to fortify your psyche and body in manners that can profit you in your regular daily existence.

Care

In view of the degrees of stress, tension and overpower that individuals regularly involvement with PTSD, discovering time for petition, reflection, and different care methods can be useful to quiet our bodies and minds.3☐ If the idea of this is awkward for you, remember that there is no strain to perform.

Simply starting with a couple of minutes out of each day of calm care can feel like a triumph. The objective of that time is to remain centered around the present with no risk of dread or judgment. Bit by bit include additional time as you go, offering yourself minutes to encounter a feeling of quiet and figure out how to adjust yourself on the off chance that you start to feel overpowered or on edge.

Exercise

Similarly as it is imperative to figure out how to quiet your psyche, it is additionally essential to get your body going. Setting aside effort to appreciate the outside, get some natural air, and move our bodies can be a useful method to direct state of mind and feelings. Research has demonstrated that physical exercise can enable our cerebrums to all the more likely adapt to stress.4☐ truth be told, analysts recommend that only a 10-minute walk every day can offer advantage to our state of mind and help to ease tension and sorrow. Here are a few things to remember as you begin:

Discover a movement you appreciate

Set little objectives

Be steady

Tune in to music or web recordings while you
work out

Request that a companion go along with you

Show restraint toward yourself

Drink a lot of liquids

Try to dress for the climate

Partake in Counseling

Conversing with an expert, for example, an instructor or specialist may feel somewhat scary, yet can be useful when you are battling with PTSD.5☐

Having a prepared individual accessible to offer help and direction in your recuperation is a key component to long haul achievement. Discover somebody you feel great with, that you find reliable and educated, and be steady in going to your sessions.

Guiding workplaces can offer a protected, quiet space for you to process with no dread of performing or be judged. Being reliable in your cooperation is useful to expand on your advancement, keep developing, and discover mending.

Keep a Journal

A few people think that its unwinding to diary their musings and have a steady spot to return to so as to compose and process their encounters. Research has indicated that individuals battling with PTSD can discover advantage in keeping a diary, including diminishing flashbacks, bad dreams and meddling recollections, helping them gradually reconnect to individuals and spots that they may somehow need to avoid.6☐ Journaling can likewise help in your directing, as you can ordinarily carry your diary to sessions as things come up that you might want to process. Chat with your specialist and check whether this may be a possibility for you.

Work

Individuals with PTSD miss more days at work and work less efficiently.7□ Certain manifestations of PTSD, for example, trouble concentrating and issues resting, may make it difficult for you to focus at work, remain sorted out, or make it to chip away at time.

Individuals with PTSD have higher paces of joblessness than individuals without PTSD. In like manner, individuals with PTSD frequently have issues at school and are more averse to endure secondary school or school.

To help explore a portion of the difficulties that PTSD can bring into the work environment, it tends to be useful for you to chat with your boss about things that could help. Being happy to convey is important for individuals to more readily comprehend your experience and to assist you with working around difficulties that you are confronting.

Case of things to make reference to might include:

Requesting adaptability with planning

Help in limiting interruptions

Minutes to regroup on the off chance that you start to feel overpowered

Revamping your work space such that causes you have a sense of security

Converse with your HR office about conceivable Employee Assistance Programs

Connections

Individuals with PTSD are bound to have issues in their relationships than individuals without PTSD.8☐ Partners of individuals with the condition might be looked with various stressors that accompany thinking about and living with somebody with enthusiastic difficulties like that of PTSD. The wellsprings of stress incorporate monetary difficulties, overseeing side effects, managing emergencies, loss of companions, or loss of closeness. These can have a significant negative effect on a relationship.

Remember that those nearest to you may as of now remember you are battling and not comprehend what to state or how to help. That doesn't mean they couldn't care less, it essentially implies they don't have the foggiest idea what to do.

At the point when we are encountering manifestations like those of PTSD, it can feel like we are totally isolated from individuals and experiencing the experience alone.

Speak the truth About Your Needs

Set aside effort to enable your friends and family to comprehend what you are encountering and speak the truth about how they can help. Request that they show restraint toward you and make sure to show restraint toward yourself too. Defining and keeping up sound limits around time or individual space can be significant seeing someone. Figuring out how to believe individuals and requesting help can be noteworthy obstructions, however are significant—particularly with the individuals who care for us most.

Cut Out Time

Feeling secluded we would say is a major piece of managing PTSD. Moving ceaselessly from individuals, closing down, or staying escaped notable individuals in our lives can prompt increasingly enthusiastic torment and all the more weakening side effects. Set aside some effort to go through with friends and family and work on imparting space to them, associating, and reconnecting. Supporting these associations via cutting out time to spend together is useful for the relationship and valuable to your recuperation and mending.

Triggers

On the off chance that you are battling with PTSD, it's conceivable that you Having PTSD likewise seems to raise dangers for unfortunate practices (for instance, smoking, absence of activity, and expanded liquor use) which may further build the plausibility of physical wellbeing problems.11 □

Getting Professional Help

Learning sound and powerful adapting aptitudes can assist you with carrying on with a more full life and deal with a portion of the side effects you are encountering with PTSD. In any case, it is imperative to likewise look for help from a certified proficient who can assist you with advancing toward recuperation and mending.

There are various compelling medicines for PTSD and treating PTSD can prompt enhancements in different parts of your life. For instance, when individuals effectively treat their PTSD, they regularly locate that different issue leave also (in spite of the fact that their different conditions may require explicit, directed medications).

Lamentably, just somewhat in excess of 33% of individuals with PTSD are in some sort of treatment.

You can locate an emotional wellness supplier for PTSD in a few different ways. Request suggestions from your family specialist, your medical coverage supplier, or those you have associated with who additionally have PTSD. On the off chance that you are a veteran, all VA Medical Centers give PTSD care. The military has programs for its individuals and their families.

Chapter 5 How to deal with the trauma

It's normal to be apprehensive in the wake of something frightening or hazardous occurs. At the point when you feel you're in risk, your body reacts with a surge of synthetic compounds that make you increasingly alert. This is known as the "flight or battle" reaction. It causes us endure perilous occasions.

Be that as it may, the cerebrum's reaction to terrifying occasions can likewise prompt constant issues. This can incorporate issue dozing; feeling nervous habitually; being effectively alarmed, on edge, or jittery; having flashbacks; or maintaining a strategic distance from things that help you to remember the occasion.

In some cases these side effects leave following half a month. However, now and again they last any longer. On the off chance that indications last over a month and become serious enough to meddle with connections or work, it might be an indication of post-awful pressure issue, or PTSD.

"There are genuine neurobiological results of injury that are related with PTSD," clarifies Dr. Farris Tuma, who directs the NIH awful pressure research program. NIH-supported scientists are revealing the science behind these mind changes and searching for approaches to counteract and treat PTSD.

What is Trauma?

"A great many people partner post-awful pressure side effects with veterans and battle circumstances," says Dr. Amit Etkin, a NIH-subsidized emotional wellness master at Stanford University. "Notwithstanding, a wide range of injury occur during one's life that can prompt post-horrible pressure issue and post-awful pressure issue like manifestations."

This incorporates individuals who have experienced a physical or rape, misuse, a mishap, a catastrophe, or numerous different genuine occasions.

Anybody can create PTSD, at any age. As per the National Center for Post-Traumatic Stress Disorder, around 7 or 8 out of each 100 individuals will encounter PTSD sooner or later in their lives.

"We don't have a blood test that would let you know or inquiry you can pose to someone to know whether they're in the most elevated hazard bunch for creating PTSD," Tuma says. "However, we do realize that there are a few things that expansion chance by and large and a few things that secure against it."

Science of Traumatic Stress

Analysts are investigating what puts individuals in danger for PTSD. One group, drove by Dr. Samuel McLean, an injury master at the University of North Carolina, is examining how post-horrible pressure side effects create in the cerebrum. They will pursue 5,000 injury survivors for one year.

"We're enlisting individuals who visit injury focuses following an injury since proof proposes that a great deal of the significant natural changes that lead to steady side effects occur in the early fallout of the injury," McLean says.

They're gathering data about existence history preceding injury, distinguishing post-awful side effects, gathering hereditary and different kinds of organic information, and performing mind filters. The examination is additionally utilizing keen watches and PDA applications to gauge the body's reaction to injury. These devices will assist scientists with revealing how injury influences individuals' day by day lives, for example, their action, rest, and state of mind.

"Our objective is that there will be when injury survivors come in for consideration and get screening and mediations to avert PTSD, just similarly that they would be screened with X-beams to set broken bones," McLean clarifies.

Adapting To Trauma

How you respond when something awful occurs, and in the blink of an eye a short time later, can help or defer your recuperation.

"It's imperative to have an adapting methodology for overcoming the awful sentiments of a horrible mishap," Tuma says. A decent adapting methodology, he clarifies, is discovering someone to converse with about your emotions. A terrible adapting system would turn liquor or medications.

Having a positive adapting procedure and taking in something from the circumstance can assist you with recuperating from a horrible accident. So can looking for help from companions, family, or a care group.

Chatting with an emotional well-being proficient can assist somebody with post-horrendous pressure side effects figure out how to adapt. It's significant for anybody with PTSD-like side effects to be treated by a psychological well-being proficient who is prepared in injury centered treatment.

A self improvement site and applications created by the U.S. Branch of Veterans Affairs can likewise offer help when you need it following an injury.

"For the individuals who start treatment and experience it, an enormous level of those will show signs of improvement and will get some help," Tuma says. A few drugs can help treat certain indications, as well.

PTSD influences individuals in an unexpected way, so a treatment that works for one individual may not work for another. A few people with PTSD need to attempt various medications to discover what works for their manifestations.

Discovering Treatments

"While we right now analyze this as one issue in psychiatry, in truth, there's a great deal of variety among individuals and the sorts of side effects that they have," Etkin says.

These distinctions can make it hard to discover a treatment that works. Etkin's group is attempting to comprehend why a few people's minds react to treatment and others don't.

"PTSD is extremely normal. In any case, the assortment of ways that it shows in the mind is huge," Etkin clarifies. "We don't have the foggiest idea what number of fundamental conditions there are, or particular mind issues there are, that lead to PTSD. So we're attempting to make sense of that part."

His group has recognized cerebrum circuits that show when treatment is working. They've discovered a different cerebrum circuit that can anticipate who will react to treatment.

His gathering is presently trying a procedure called noninvasive cerebrum incitement for individuals who don't react to treatment. They trust that animating certain mind circuits will make treatment progressively compelling.

A great many people recoup normally from injury. Be that as it may, it can require significant investment. In case you're having indications for a really long time—or that are excessively extreme—chat with your medicinal services supplier or a psychological wellness proficient. In the midst of emergency, call the National Suicide Prevention Lifeline at 1-800-273-TALK (8255) or visit the crisis room.

"PTSD is genuine. This isn't a shortcoming in any capacity," Tuma clarifies. "Individuals shouldn't battle alone and peacefully."

Chapter 6 - Dealing with category D symptoms

Sufficient endurance conduct is a vital "endowment of nature." Humans have been genuinely effective in lessening the danger to life. All things considered, going across a road or driving a vehicle requires expanded readiness so as to endure. Cataclysmic events, for example, the ongoing tidal wave and man-made calamities, for example, war, fear monger assaults, slaughtering, looting, sexual and physical maltreatment, and plane accidents show how helpless we are. In the wake of enduring such an occasion, individuals need nuts and bolts—nourishment, cover, therapeutic consideration, and encouragement. These days mental consideration has been added to this rundown of fundamental requirements for certain individuals.

Specialists should know whether and when mental assistance is vital. The new rule on overseeing post-horrible pressure issue in essential and auxiliary consideration from the National Institute for Clinical Excellence (NICE) fantastically outlines the encounters of sufferers and carers and gives proof and exhortation on intercessions for grown-ups and children.1 The rule gives extraordinary thoughtfulness regarding "debacle arranging"; the requirements of ex-military staff, casualties of abusive behavior at home, and displaced people and refuge searchers; and the job of the non-statutory segment, underscoring the expansive effect of injury in present day society. Giving more regard for the nature and importance of post-awful pressure issue in a social and recorded setting would have made the rules total.

At the point when manifestations, for example, flashbacks, rest issues, trouble in concentrating, and passionate lability are gentle and have been available for under about a month after horrible mishaps, the rules suggest beginning attentive pausing. Behind this shrewd counsel lies the proof based end that early mental intercession, frequently called questioning, has no impact in anticipating post-horrendous stress issue; for sure, regardless of detailed high fulfillment, it may even be harmful.2-4 Clearly the standard practice of questioning after debacles and fiascoes should end. In any case, for dealing with the bedlam, material misfortunes, misery, and outrage—for instance, after a fear based oppressor assault—no indisputable proof is accessible yet on how a fiasco stricken network recovers control.

As per the NICE rule, treatment is essential when, in the outcome of injury, post-horrible pressure issue, misery, suicidality, compulsion, restoratively unexplained physical side effects, or dissociative issue emerge. The danger of creating post-horrendous pressure issue after injury is 8-13% for men and 20-30% for women,5 with a year pervasiveness of 1.3% to 3.9%,6 making a colossal weight on society.

Post-horrendous pressure issue is essentially a deregulation of the dread framework. Dread is an essential feeling on occasion of peril, and is trailed by a stress reaction—battling, solidifying, or escaping. This endurance framework relies upon evaluating dangers so as to start endurance behaviour.7 Once the risk or injury is finished, the dread framework ordinarily quiets down following a couple of days or weeks. In post-awful pressure issue this framework neglects to reset to typical, keeping the sufferer hyperalert, filtering for hazardous signals as though the occasion may happen once more.

The turmoil is subsequently described by automatic, tireless recalling or remembering the awful accident in flashbacks, striking recollections, and intermittent dreams. The individual attempts to abstain from recalling the injury, by dodging its area or TV programs about it. Diligent manifestations of expanded excitement, for example, hypervigilance, overstated frighten reaction, dozing issues, peevishness, and trouble concentrating, are a piece of the turmoil. Comorbidities, for example, misery, substance misuse, and other nervousness issue are the standard instead of the exemption. Passionate desensitizing, for example, feeling isolates from others, is likewise observed—for instance in officers subsequent to peacekeeping missions.

The NICE rule deliberately audits the proof for both mental and pharmacological mediations. As first line treatment NICE suggests injury centered mental treatment. Both distributed and unpublished information demonstrate just constrained viability for few pharmacological intercessions, so NICE prescribes not utilizing drugs as first line treatment.

The best treatment for resetting the dread framework is psychological conduct therapy.8 By fanciful presentation to the horrendous accident the dread response will diminish in time. Ideas about the self that are provoked by the occasion, for example, feeling "frail," liable, or insusceptible, are supplanted by progressively sensible perceptions. The rule likewise underpins, yet not as unequivocally, treatment with eye development desensitization reprocessing, which uses a distractive move of respective incitement after presentation to diminish the passionate lability identified with the injury.

An unanswered inquiry remains whether the elevated feeling of dread in post-horrendous stress issue is identified with the occasion or to the concealment of bizarrely compelling feelings of despondency and animosity realized by the awful experience.9 Like Summerfield we accept that more consideration ought to be paid to the significance of shocking encounters, breaking the sufferer's perspectives about life,10 in spite of the fact that proof on this viewpoint is deficient. We additionally concur with the rule about focusing on the regular comorbidities of post-awful pressure issue, (for example, misery and uneasiness), however the proof is still very limited.1

Regardless of the presence of powerful psychosocial medications, 33% of patients won't recuperate fully.11 Comorbidity, chronicity, and the aggregation of intense and ceaseless pressure may disclose the restricted reaction to treatment. Additionally, from a developmental perspective one can perceive how "the endowment of nature" of recollecting and gaining from peril may confine what is achievable in treating post-horrendous pressure disorder.12 We can't erase the memory of injury.

Chapter 7   What to do if you can't sleep, can't relax, or are angry and irritable

Outrage and post-horrible pressure issue (PTSD) frequently happen together. Normal in this condition, outrage is one of the hyperarousal side effects of PTSD and it might influence associations with individuals around you. It's imperative to realize that the annoyance of individuals with PTSD can turn out to be exceptional to such an extent that it feels wild. At the point when that occurs, you may get forceful toward others or even mischief yourself. That doesn't generally occur, be that as it may, and not every person with PTSD lashes out irately. Remember that outrage is just a single indication of PTSD; truth be told, it is anything but a prerequisite for accepting a PTSD diagnosis.1□ Although it very well may be, It's not constantly fierce, either. As a general rule, somebody with PTSD who will in general feel extraordinary outrage attempts to drive it down or conceal it from others. This can prompt pointless conduct.

How about we investigate outrage in PTSD. There are various circumstances where it will in general happen and a few different ways to help monitor it that you will discover accommodating.

Hyperarousal Symptoms of PTSD

Youthful representative looking focused

Andy Smith/Getty Images

Outrage and touchiness are hyperarousal side effects of PTSD. Consider hyperarousal a steady condition of "battle or flight." This elevated uneasiness can have an assortment of side effects including trouble resting, touchiness, and hypervigilance.2☐ There are, in any case, approaches to adapt to each of these.

Productive and Destructive Anger in PTSD

Two youngsters having a contention in an office

Individuals frequently principally view outrage as a negative or hurtful feeling. Be that as it may, that is not generally the situation. The facts confirm that outrage can frequently prompt unfortunate practices like substance misuse or indiscreet activities. However, feeling furious isn't "awful" in itself. It's a substantial enthusiastic encounter and it can give you significant data.

You may have heard annoyance characterized into two kinds: helpful indignation and damaging resentment. Productive outrage can help with recuperating, progress ahead, and recuperation, while ruinous outrage can cause harm.☐ It's a smart thought to comprehend this distinction and discover methods for overseeing both in your life.

11 Ways to Calm Yourself Fast When You're Really Mad

Outrage and PTSD in Combat Veterans

Stressed man sitting on couch utilizing wireless

The contentions in Iraq and Afghanistan have shown us more their effect on people in military assistance. It's become evident that veterans are in danger for various emotional wellness issues, including PTSD and outrageous annoyance.

However, it's critical to recollect that you are not the only one in this. There are an assortment of treatment alternatives accessible and different vets that are feeling a similar way. The more we find out about PTSD in veterans, the more we are finding out about powerful treatments, and more assistance individuals are discovering help.4☐

For what reason Is There Such a High Percentage of PTSD in the Military?

PTSD and Relationship Violence

In the event that your relationship is influenced by PTSD, it's insightful to find out about the relationship among it and brutality. While the two are associated, not every person with PTSD is or will manhandle their accomplice. Notwithstanding, in the event that you or somebody you know is a casualty of relationship viciousness, it's imperative to know there are assets accessible. Lamentably, inquire about has discovered an association among PTSD and relationship brutality. On a yearly premise, somewhere in the range of 8 and 21 percent of individuals in genuine personal connections take forceful activities against their accomplices.

Pointless Behaviors in PTSD

Miserable lady in bistro watching out of window

Albeit exceptional annoyance can make individuals with PTSD be forceful toward others, as a rule they'll attempt to push down or shroud their outrage. This can be compelling temporarily, however in the long haul, it can develop the outrage until it's crazy. At the point when that occurs, a few people turn their displeasure on themselves as reckless practices. This may incorporate substance misuse or purposeful self-harm.5 While this is regular with PTSD, there are approaches to adapt to it that you'll need to know.

Types of Self-Harm Common in People With PTSD

Outrage Management Techniques

lady sitting on love seat at home ruminating

As you most likely know, outrage can be a troublesome feeling to oversee, particularly in the event that it feels serious and wild. Instead of going to undesirable practices to attempt to alleviate or overlook it, it's a smart thought to learn valuable resentment the board techniques. Incorporated into these are basic things like exercise, rehearsing care, and discovering somebody you trust to work things out with. Now and again, it can appear to be a lengthy, difficult experience. In the end, something may snap and you'll locate a couple of procedures that work for your life.

How Anger Can Affect Your Health

Taking a Time-Out from Anger

Agent at workstation watching out window

Inside those helpful displeasure the executives abilities is the recommendation to take a "break" when you feel yourself beginning to get angry. It's a simple aptitude to learn.

At the point when you build up a break plan, you give yourself explicit strides to take when you feel outrage. Numerous individuals with PTSD have discovered this an extraordinary hotspot for alleviation and an amazing methodology for their connections.

Utilizing Self-Soothing Skills for Anger

lady holding container of basic oil

Have you caught wind of utilizing self-alleviating abilities to help deal with your anger?7☐ They're anything but difficult to learn and utilize on the grounds that they're intended to make you feel much improved, and you do them all alone. Self-alleviating aptitudes utilize your five detects—contact, taste, smell, sight, and sound. The key is to concentrate on the movement. By staying careful about an option that is other than your displeasure, your psyche and body normally become more settled.

Searching out Social Support

bunch treatment session

Conversing with others as a method for "getting your feelings out" can be compelling in keeping outrage from working up inside.7☐ For a certain something, it can assist you with seeing someone else's perspective. It additionally offers you the chance to express your disappointments in a productive manner. Obviously, it's critical to ensure that you contact individuals you believe who will comprehend and bolster your emotions. Care groups for PTSD are broadly accessible and numerous individuals have seen them as an incredible assistance with their own difficulties.

Nervousness Management Skills

lady breathing with eyes shut

In all honesty, adapting aptitudes for overseeing nervousness can likewise help deal with your outrage successfully. Why? Since exceptional indignation and tension are comparable feelings in that both will in general touch off a "battle or flight" response.At the point when you learn abilities for adapting to exceptional tension, you're likewise learning approaches to keep your resentment at less serious levels. Keep in mind that your PTSD triggers may incite either feeling, so it merits your opportunity to pick up adapting aptitudes for both.

Chapter 8 The close relationship between stress, trauma and body

Studies have indicated that constant torment may not exclusively be brought about by physical damage yet in addition by stress and intense subject matters. Specifically, individuals who have encountered injury and experience the ill effects of Post Traumatic Stress Disorder (PTSD) are frequently at a higher hazard to create incessant torment.

Ceaseless agony is characterized as delayed physical torment that goes on for longer than the characteristic mending procedure ought to permit. This agony may originate from wounds, irritation, or neuralgias and neuropathies (issue of the nerves), yet a few people endure without any of these conditions. Interminable torment can incapacitate one's capacity to move effortlessly, may obstruct their ordinary working, and the quest for alleviation can prompt torment medicine addictions, which aggravate the issue. Ceaseless agony is likewise frequently joined by sentiments of sadness, wretchedness and uneasiness.

Numerous individuals are now acquainted with the way that enthusiastic pressure can prompt stomachaches, bad tempered gut disorder, and migraines, however probably won't realize that it can likewise cause other physical grievances and even incessant agony. One sensible explanation behind this: thinks about have discovered that the more on edge and focused on individuals are, the more tense and choked their muscles are, after some time making the muscles become exhausted and wasteful.

All the more unpretentiously, one may create psychosomatic side effects or stress-related indications as a result of uncertain intense subject matters. These are not new disclosures; specialists have considered the psyche/body interrelationship for a very long while as a result of the significance of this connection.

Specialists have seen that encountering an awful accident can affect the improvement of torment. Truth be told, around 15-30% of patients with constant torment additionally have PTSD. Dwindle Levine, a specialist on injury, clarifies that injury happens "when our capacity to react to an apparent danger is here and there overpowering." Most analysts differ on an exact meaning of injury, however concur that an average injury reaction may incorporate physiological and mental manifestations, for example, desensitizing, hyperarousal, hypervigilance, bad dreams, flashbacks, weakness, and shirking conduct.

During an awful accident, the sensory system goes into endurance mode (the thoughtful sensory system) and in some cases experiences issues returning into its ordinary, loosened up mode once more (the parasympathetic sensory system). In the event that the sensory system remains in endurance mode, stress hormones, for example, cortisol are continually discharged, causing an expansion in circulatory strain and glucose, which can thus decrease the invulnerable framework's capacity to recuperate. Physical indications begin to show when the body is in consistent trouble.

In the event that somebody has encountered an injury preceding their present damage or injury, old recollections can conceivably be activated, compounding the impacts of the more current injury. Dr. Bessel van der Kolk, an outstanding injury specialist, clarifies; "Exploration has indicated that, under normal conditions, many damaged individuals, including assault unfortunate casualties, battered ladies and mishandled youngsters, have a genuinely decent psychosocial modification. In any case, they don't react to pressure the manner in which other individuals do. Under strain, they may feel (or go about) as though they were damaged once more."

Frequently, physical agony capacities to caution an individual that there is as yet passionate work to be done, and it can likewise be an indication of uncertain injury in the sensory system. Regardless of whether one has lamented and prepared the enthusiastic effect of an injury, the sensory system may even now accidentally be in endurance mode.

Maggie Phillips, writer of Reversing Chronic Pain, expresses: "Regardless of whether injury was associated with the occasion or condition that began their agony, having a ceaseless torment condition is damaging all by itself."

Since injury has been found to have a solid connection to ceaseless agony, a blend of psychotherapy and exercise based recuperation would be the most sensible torment the executives choice for stress and incessant help with discomfort. Psychotherapy that utilizations symbolism, addresses the sensory system, and encourages subjective conduct treatment is suggested.

To handle the physical part of interminable torment, Mindy Marantz, executive of the Healthwell center in San Francisco, recommends concentrating on arrangement in the body, just as stance that supports sorted out arrangement. Also, she encourages to address potential aggravation, and gives techniques to help quiet the sensory system, for example, Craniosacral treatment or Feldenkrais Movement Re-instruction. "These both will help 'stir' the lymphatic framework, which thus lessens the impacts of liquids that pool because of damage. Lymphatic rub just as pressure wraps and instruction help carry this regularly ignored pathway to recuperation to patients' consideration."

Starting an every day program of strolling can prepare the muscles and is the most ideal approach to animate the lymph framework to carry out its responsibility and oxygenate harmed muscles. The International Association for the Study of Pain reasoned that needle therapy is likewise viable in long haul interminable torment decreases identified with musculoskeletal agony.

Albeit one probably won't know about the waiting impact of the injury, or accept that the horrendous accident has been put behind them, the body could be sticking to uncertain issues. Significant psychotherapy can resolve the physical issues.

Chapter 9 For veterans returning from war: tools for personal survival.

US veterans are multifaceted and might be viewed as a populace, a culture, and a subculture. Military culture incorporates, yet isn't constrained to, the qualities, traditions, conventions, philosophical standards, ethos, measures of conduct, guidelines of control, cooperation, devotion, caring obligation, rank, character, chain of command, service and behavior, union, request and methodology, sets of principles, understood examples of correspondence, and dutifulness to order (LD Purnell, University of Delaware and Florida International University, individual correspondence, January, 2015). The American veteran populace is a remarkable populace. Shifting military assistance branches and fluctuating military encounters among the veteran populace is one of a kind. Differing wartime times and wellbeing explicit issues related with those times are special among the veteran populace. From an examination of veterans from the Vietnam, Persian Gulf, and Iraq/Afghanistan (Operation Iraqi Freedom [OIF]/Operation Enduring Freedom [OEF]) war times, Fontana and Rosenheck2 noted unmistakable contrasts. OIF/OEF veterans incorporate less African-Americans, more Latinos, and a bigger number of females than different periods. What's more, this gathering is more youthful, more averse to be hitched, less inclined to have been detained, and bound to be beneficially employed.2 It was additionally seen that OIF/OEF veterans seem, by all accounts, to be all the more socially coordinated, less regularly determined to have substance misuse issue, and required less Veterans Affairs (VA) incapacity pay for post-horrible pressure issue (PTSDs) when contrasted with their Persian Gulf and Vietnam veteran counterparts.

US veteran-explicit medical problems

Emotional well-being or conduct change issue

Therapeutic records of veterans uncover "that one of every three patients was determined to have at any rate one psychological wellness issue – 41% were determined to have either an emotional well-being or a conduct modification disorder". In remuneration or in mix with military-related infections, numerous veterans create substance use issue (SUDs) and an enormous number eventually end it all. LeardMann et al4 found that male veterans determined to have "sadness, hyper burdensome issue, substantial or hard-core boozing, and liquor related issues" were fundamentally connected with an expanded danger of suicide. Along these lines, recognizing and treating emotional well-being sickness has the best potential to moderate suicide chance. Shockingly, hesitance to look for help or treatment makes diagnosing and treating psychological sickness troublesome in this populace.

SUDs

The stressors of military assistance increment the danger of veterans having issues with liquor, tobacco, or drugs (or a mix). Johnson et al5 found that cigarette smoking and liquor utilization is higher among veterans than non-military staff. For certain veterans, treatment of a co-horrible condition (eg, PTSD, melancholy, torment, a sleeping disorder) may resolve the issue. For other people, long haul care is required. In this manner, various clinical practice rules have been created "and proof based screening apparatuses to assist clinicians with distinguishing veterans with SUDs and improve outcomes".

PTSD

Otherwise called "shell stun" or "battle exhaustion", PTSD comes about because of seeing or encountering (straightforwardly or by implication) a horrible event. The ailment isn't restricted to veterans, be that as it may, military work force experience PTSD right around four overlap (8% of non-military men versus 36% of male veterans). PTSD is an amalgam of side effects, seriousness, and span. As per the American Psychiatric Association, conclusion depends on four indication classifications: nosy manifestations (flashbacks), evasion of updates (detachment), negative considerations and sentiments ("nobody can be trusted"), and excitement and reactivity side effects (overstated surprise reaction). PTSD is frequently connected with "horrible cerebrum damage (TBI), military sexual injury (MST), rest issues, substance use, torment, and other mental issue, and requires exhaustive assessment". Treatment is gone for treatment (psychotherapy, delayed introduction treatment, family/bunch treatment, and others), social help, as well as prescription, for example, antidepressants. Screening instruments and proof-based rules have been created to precisely and speedily evaluate and treat veterans.

TBI

TBI is "horrendously actuated auxiliary damage as well as physiological disturbance of cerebrum work because of an outer force".TBI can be named gentle, moderate, or extreme relying upon the length of obviousness, memory misfortune/confusion, and responsiveness of the individual after the occasion (ie, are they ready to pursue directions). While mellow TBI (or blackout) is the most widely recognized, finding is troublesome since manifestations incorporate "migraines, tipsiness/issues strolling, exhaustion, touchiness, memory issues and issues paying attention".

Misery

Among the accessible information from the National Alliance on Mental Illness (NAMI),2 misery positions among the most widely recognized emotional wellness issue. The analysis rate for veteran gloom is 14% (in spite of the fact that NAMI accepts despondency is under analyzed). Remarkably, NAMI2 found that people with PTSD were less inclined to end it all versus those with melancholy most likely because of the expanded mindfulness and acknowledgment of PTSD. In spite of its overwhelming impacts, significant melancholy is a treatable ailment with 80%–90% achievement rate utilizing medicine, psychotherapy, and additionally electroconvulsive therapy. Models of care, for example, Translating Initiatives for Depression into Effective Solutions, show eight out of ten veterans are viably treated.

Suicide

With 18 to 22 veterans ending it all every day, chance evaluation and intercession are paramount.9 Private and general medicinal services experts must know about patients' military history (since not all veterans look for care in VA clinics)5 and have the option to perceive suicide-chance components, paying little respect to age. Youthful veterans matured 18–44 years are most in danger of suicide; yet, Kemp and Bossarte9 found that much more seasoned veterans, matured 50 years and more established, were still twice as liable to end it all versus non-veterans (69% and 37%, individually). Furthermore, "11% of veterans who endure a first suicide endeavor will reattempt inside 9 months, and 6% of those will die".5 Kemp and Bossarte9 discovered proof supporting the viability of VA social insurance frameworks in bringing down veterans' non-deadly suicide endeavor rate, hence referral to a VA office is suggested for suitable directing and wellbeing administrations.

Constant torment

With 82% of OEF and OIF veterans detailing interminable agony, finding and treatment are essential.5 A complete appraisal of torment is urgent, yet in addition distinguishing related physiological/natural and mental variables since "constant physical torment is frequently connected with co-sullen conditions, including TBI and PTSD, that may convolute treatment".5,7 Treatment should concentrate on simultaneously tending to all conditions, with outrageous preventative utilization of narcotics because of the elevated danger of veterans creating SUDs.

Removals

Progression in medicinal innovation and substantial insurance enable troopers to endure wounds at a higher rate than in past wars. However, the scars from a horrible removal are profound and numerous officers create emotional well-being wounds identified with the occasion and "in cases including different appendage removals or deformation, self-perception issues may make various social and work barriers".5 According to military loss insights, 1,573 veterans have endured significant loss of appendage removals from fight wounds since 2010.10

Medicinal services experts must have the option to address the physical wellbeing worries, just as, the passionate soundness of the veteran. Tactile guides, prosthesis, and restorative recovery require an interdisciplinary-group approach in recuperating injured fighters.

Restoration care

Numerous veterans experience serious difficulties reacclimating into society after organization because of military aptitudes that are not transferrable to regular citizen life, substantial injury that rendered that individual crippled, as well as war-related mental sickness. Recovery care is gone for a parity of professional, physical, social, and mental treatments to get ready veterans for reemergence into nonmilitary personnel life. Professional projects help work looking for veterans create abilities and information required for a specific work. Physical recovery centers around improving veterans' personal satisfaction and freedom. Social restoration helps veterans to absorb to non-military life and set up better approaches forever post-arrangement. Mental recovery shows veterans with emotional well-being disease the living aptitudes of network working and capacity to manage their new condition.

Dangerous exposures

Veterans' past introduction to synthetic substances (Agent Orange, defiled water), radiation (atomic weapons, X-beams), air toxins (consume pit smoke, dust), word related dangers (asbestos, lead), fighting specialists (concoction and natural weapons), clamor, and vibration increment their danger of medical issues even a long time after the underlying assault.11 For instance, long haul medical issues have been ensnared in relationship with Agent Orange presentation in Vietnam veterans.12 For the individuals who served in Iraq and Afghanistan, there is deficient information to distinguish long haul wellbeing impacts of perilous introduction to contaminations, for example, "consume pits" and irresistible operators, for example, rabies, in spite of the quick reactions experienced by most veterans.5 Obtaining a precise restorative and organization history is basic in giving exact determination and suitable treatment.

Vagrancy

It is evaluated that around 49,933 veterans are destitute (~12% of destitute grown-up population).13 Homeless veterans face indistinguishable troubles from non-veterans, for example, substance use, joblessness, and dysfunctional behavior; yet tormented with the extra weights of military tensions.

Chapter 10 - There is a reason for everything

Story of a business man

Some time prior, I left a business. Regardless I recall the inclination when I did it. I was overwhelmed with this impression of ill will and coerce. I was immersed tragically and despair. I had gone through three years constructing that business and it could have effectively become a 9-figure realm at the absolute minimum. In any case, I left.

At the point when I did, I truly addressed in the case of everything occurs in life which is as it should be. Yet, some place, in the back of my brain, I heard the voice of God. I realized that no one but He could transform a wreck into a message, a test into a declaration, a preliminary into a triumph and an injured individual into a triumph. I knew there must be an explanation behind everything. I just couldn't discover it at the time. Whenever we fizzle at something, we're overwhelmed by a feeling of thrashing. It's tendency. Furthermore, it's a piece of life. We as a whole experience it. Does it feel better? Not a chance. Not in the scarcest. In any case, you can't generally anticipate that life should be rainbows and daylight. Yet, there is a purpose behind the things that transpire. Truth be told, the best exercises you would ever take in life are conceived from disappointment.

I feel that time and again, individuals are so scared of disappointment that they burn through the majority of their lives running from it, when, indeed, it ought to be grasped and invited. You will never gain from progress. You will never improve in case you're continually living on the good life. There is genuine quality and progress to increase only outside of your usual range of familiarity.

All things considered, I realize this doesn't make it feel any better. I can just relate the voyage. I can just pass on how it feels. I can relate the agony and help other people find courses through it. I can't improve it. Nobody can. In any case, through the torment of disappointment and our most trying encounters, something great is conceived. It's a reestablishment of soul, a birth of restoration and a general faith in more prominent what might be on the horizon.

In the event that you have confidence in God, Allah, Buddha, or just the all inclusive unity that ties all of us, you've likely understood that everything in life happens on purpose. What's more, in any event, when you can't comprehend it at that exact second, it does. Since, down the line, some place later on, some place in the obscure, something different happens that is great to the point, that it's at exactly that point that you understand it would have never worked out as expected had you not endured that previous disaster in any case.

"Find the #1 aptitude that will give you an unjustifiable preferred position throughout everyday life and enable you to accomplish any objective on autopilot!" Click here to download my quick activity cheatsheet at the present time.

Why Things Happen For a Reason

In the event that you're enduring a disaster at this moment, at that point my heart goes out to you. I know the sentiment of despondency very well. Perhaps I'm only an incredibly touchy individual, however it influences me profoundly. However, of course, disappointment and disaster influences everybody. It may affect us in an unexpected way, however by the day's end, it impacts us.

Be that as it may, there's a motivation behind why those things transpire. Disappointment and disaster are by plan. They are a piece of nature's etch, wearing down us trying to improve our lives. Be that as it may, it doesn't occur by lounging around and feeling frustrated about yourself. You need to transform that wreckage into a message. You probably won't understand it today, however there is a fantastic structure. At the point when I left that business, there was one thing experiencing my brain. Everything I could consider was the way that people were intended to flourish, not simply endure. I was living in endurance mode. Rationally and genuinely and even profoundly, I was on endurance autopilot. I was attempting to endure the feelings that had inundated me and modified my point of view.

However, I understood that this experience and this circumstance was intended for me to flourish. What's more, flourish I have. It's interesting how things can truly change your direction on the off chance that you grasp them as opposed to run from them. I was put here which is as it should be. I was intended to help other people understand the utility in their disappointments and not to run from them. Indeed, there are different explanations behind my reality, yet that is positively one of the foundations.

What had befallen me was that I was getting further and further away from helping other people. I was so drenched in my own sh*t that I couldn't see the famous woods through the trees. In any case, since that experience, some remarkable things have transpired.

For quite a while, I had disregarded systems administration and building profound and enduring associations with individuals. In any case, after that experience, I suffocated myself in helping other people. I made enormous incentive for others without anybody consistently requesting that I do as such. I constructed spans, not dividers. Presently, on the off chance that you need to go ahead throughout everyday life, at that point that is actually what you have to do. Since, by including an incentive in this world, and by helping other people make their very own progress, you structure the most profound and longest-enduring bonds.

Truly, everything happens for an explanation throughout everyday life. Everything. We probably won't understand it. In any case, it does. Furthermore, they do. Be that as it may, there are 5 basic reasons why I feel that everything occurs for an explanation throughout everyday life. These 5 reasons are crucial to our more noteworthy comprehension of the significance of our lives. No, I'm making an effort not to get existential on you here. I'm being not kidding.

#1 — It sets you up for what's to come

One very incredible acknowledgment is that everything occurs for an explanation since it's setting you up for what's to come throughout everyday life. It's preparing you for a greater and more promising time to come. You can't have the joy of progress without enduring the torment of destruction. In any event, when these are disasters outside of our control, there is an explanation behind them.

Psychologically, it doesn't bode well. I realize that. You can't comprehend the reasons why somebody passes on, somebody leaves you for another person, or why a business may crumple. All you're managing at the time is torment. In any case, when that agony washes over you, and you move gradually into the future, things start happening that wouldn't have happened had you not endured that torment in any case.

#2 — It makes you stronger

Disappointment, disaster and thrashing makes you stronger. Not when you're enduring it. Be that as it may, after some time as the weeks, months and years wear on. Regularly, you will never get over those greatest heartbreaks throughout everyday life. In any case, that is alright. Since it shapes you into a stronger individual. It solidifies you for what's to come. In all actuality extreme occasions never last. However, extreme individuals do. What's more, the scars that we get in life will help to remember us where we've been, however they don't really need to direct where we will go. Try not to flounder excessively far in wretchedness. Lift yourself up. Discover the excellence in the straightforward things in life since that is what's significant at times. Eventually, you comprehend that not all things are in your control, nor should it be. You essentially can't control everything that transpires throughout everyday life. Be that as it may, you can control how you react. There's an old statement that says life is 10% what befalls you and 90% how you respond to it.

#3 — It causes you to break your old convictions

When something terrible happens to us, and it's inside our control, as in, the conditions were our very own result conduct, it has a major effect on our inner self. Indeed, it breaks our old convictions. We go wrong and understand that whatever it is that we were doing, anyway it is that we were carrying on, wasn't at all legitimate. You take a gander at things in an unexpected way. You figure out how to approach it in another manner. That is the thing about convictions. They're instilled in us from youth. They're prepared into our psyches. Also, it's so difficult to defeat those old convictions when we're stuck in our manners living in average quality. I'm not discussing disasters here. I'm discussing disappointments that we assumed a job in.

It's truly ground-breaking to break your old convictions. It's basically your personality smashing down to the floor. We're ready to reason such an extensive amount our restricting conduct since it's saturated with propensities. We follow delight while attempting to evade torment for the time being. Not in the long haul. In the event that we were staying away from torment in the long haul we would consistently do what it took to gain enormous ground and improve after some time.

#4 — It assists welcome with advancing not flawlessness

It's about progress and not flawlessness. Envision having the option to improve any aspect of your life by only one percent consistently. That one percent mixes on itself after some time. Be that as it may, over and over again, we don't improve. We really remain stale. That is, until we're shocked out of our old constraining examples of conduct by some profound measure of torment or disappointment. That is the point at which life's genuine exercises get going.

Be that as it may, again and again, when something turns out badly, we fall of the notorious wagon. We don't gain a tad of ground. We really go in reverse. Nonetheless, when that profound and unexpected disappointment happens, it opens your eyes to the need of gaining ground.

#5 — It makes you progressively sympathetic and genuine

It's difficult to be compassionate when you haven't generally endured significant annihilation and catastrophe. It simply is. Without a doubt, you can be thoughtful still. Yet, not sympathetic. Compassion possibly happens when you can really relate through an involvement with another person. There's genuine power in that. It likewise makes you unmistakably progressively genuine and far less shallow. It's anything but difficult to be shallow. We as a whole have 3 countenances. The face we show the world, the face we show loved ones, and our other face that we show nobody. The last is our actual self. What happens when you endure a major disaster is as a rule those faces consolidation and you are left with a substantially more obvious and genuine face.

For what reason is that significant? Since realness and straightforwardness is so difficult to find nowadays. Be that as it may, when you discover an individual who's genuine and bona fide and straightforward, it truly makes you halt abruptly. Those are the sorts of individuals that I encircle myself with. Not phony individuals who are just worried about what others consider them.

Chapter 11 - Final thoughts and exercises

Individuals with post-horrible pressure issue (PTSD) regularly battle with visit and exceptional manifestations of nervousness. These solid side effects of nervousness frequently lead individuals with PTSD to depend on undesirable methods for adapting, for example, through medication or liquor use. Luckily, there are various solid methods for adapting to nervousness that may enable your uneasiness to go down in power, become less regular, and additionally become increasingly decent.

Profound Breathing

Profound breathing can be a significant adapting expertise to learn. It might sound senseless, however numerous individuals don't inhale appropriately. Regular breathing includes your stomach, an enormous muscle in your belly. At the point when you take in, your gut ought to grow. At the point when you inhale out, your midsection should fall. After some time, individuals overlook how to inhale along these lines and rather utilize their chest and shoulders. This causes short and shallow breaths, which can build pressure and nervousness. Luckily, it isn't past the point where it is possible to "re-realize" how to inhale and help shield yourself from stress. Practice this straightforward exercise to improve your breathing and battle uneasiness.

Dynamic Muscle Relaxation

Utilizing unwinding activities can be a successful method to lessen your pressure and tension. One unwinding activity called dynamic muscle unwinding centers around an individual switching back and forth among straining and loosening up various muscle bunches all through the body. This unwinding strategy is like a pendulum. Complete unwinding of your muscles can be gotten by first setting off to the next outrageous (that is, by straining your muscles). Likewise, by straining your muscles (a typical manifestation of uneasiness) and quickly loosening up them, the side effect of muscle pressure may turn into a sign to unwind after some time. You can gain proficiency with a fundamental dynamic muscle unwinding exercise in this article.

Care

Utilizing care for uneasiness can be useful. Care has been around for a very long time. Nonetheless, psychological wellness experts are starting to perceive that care can have numerous advantages for individuals experiencing challenges, for example, nervousness and despondency. Basically, care is tied in with being in contact with and mindful of the present minute. So frequently in our lives, we are latched onto our subconscious minds, made up for lost time in the uneasiness and stresses of every day life. This activity will acquaint you with care and might be useful getting you "out of your head" and in contact with the present minute.

Self-Monitoring

Self-observing can be a useful method for understanding your tension indications. We are all "animals of propensity." We regularly approach our day without deduction, being uninformed of much that goes on around us. This might be helpful in certain circumstances, however different occasions, this absence of mindfulness may make us feel as if our considerations and feelings are totally capricious and unmanageable. We can't generally address awkward side effects of uneasiness without first monitoring what circumstances raise these sentiments. Self-observing is a basic method for expanding this mindfulness.

Social Support

Again and again, it has been discovered that discovering support from others can be a central point in helping individuals defeat the negative impacts of a horrible mishap and PTSD. Having somebody you believe that you can converse with can be exceptionally useful for working through upsetting circumstances or for passionate approval. Be that as it may, basically having somebody accessible to converse with may not be sufficient. There are a few significant pieces to a steady relationship that might be especially valuable in helping somebody deal with their nervousness.

Self-Soothing

At the point when you are encountering tension, it is imperative to have methods for adapting to those emotions. For instance, searching out social help can be an astounding method for improving your state of mind. Be that as it may, the uneasiness related with side effects of PTSD can here and there happen surprisingly, and social help may not be promptly accessible. In this manner, it is critical to pick up adapting procedures that you can do without anyone else. Adapting techniques concentrated on improving your mind-set and decreasing the tension that you can do individually are now and again depicted as self-calming or self-care adapting procedures.

Expressive Writing

Utilizing journaling to adapt to and express your contemplations and sentiments (additionally called expressive composition) can be a decent method for adapting to tension. Expressive composing has been found to improve physical and mental wellbeing. As to PTSD specifically, expressive composing has been found to have various advantages including improved adapting and posttraumatic development (or the capacity to discover importance in and have positive life changes following an awful mishap), just as decreased PTSD side effects, pressure, and outrage.

Interruption

Deliberate utilization of interruption strategies can really be of advantage in adapting to feelings that are solid and feel awkward, for example, tension and dread. Interruption is anything you do to briefly remove your consideration from forceful feeling. Some of the time, concentrating on a forceful feeling can make it feel significantly more grounded and progressively crazy. Subsequently, by incidentally diverting yourself, you may give the feeling some an opportunity to diminish in force, making it simpler to oversee.

Conduct Activation

Uneasiness and shirking go connected at the hip. While the shirking of uneasiness inciting circumstances may help diminish our tension right now, in the long haul it might keep us from carrying on with an important and compensating life (particularly as this evasion becomes greater and greater). Conduct initiation is an extraordinary method for expanding your action level, just as the amount you take part in positive and remunerating exercises. Through social actuation, you can lessen your downturn and tension.